glenn

glenn

a play by David Young

COACH HOUSE BOOKS, TORONTO

Second Edition (revised) · Third printing

A professionally produced audio component is vital to the staging of this play. Musical director Don Horsburgh has designed a wall-to-wall sound-scape to accompany the text. It consists of sampled piano cues from the Gould library mixed with sound cues appropriate to the content and context of each variation.

For information regarding permission and terms please apply to:
David Young
c/o Coach House Books
80 bpNichol Lane
Toronto, Ontario M5S 3J4
mail@chbooks.com

Author's acknowledgements: Thanks to Richard Rose, Paul Ledoux and Don Kugler for their help in the development of this play. Thanks also to the Toronto Arts Council, the Canada Council and the Ontario Arts Council for vital financial assistance. Special thanks to George D. Butterfield and Jill Fraser for their support. This project was developed with the permission of the Estate of Glenn Gould and Glenn Gould Limited.

Cover photograph courtesy of Nancy Beatty
Production stills courtesy of Cylla von Tiedemann

CANADIAN CATALOGUING IN PUBLICATION DATA
Young, David, 1946-
    Glenn
A play.
ISBN 1-55245-058-9
1. Gould, Glenn, 1932-1982 – Drama. I. Title.
PS8597.O59G54 1999   C812'.54   C99-931108-5
PR9199.3.Y58G54 1999

Art, on its loftiest mission, is hardly human at all.

– Glenn Gould

Contents

Act Two

Foreword

When I sat down to read David Young's play in the summer of 1992, I was barely past the aria and the first four or five variations when something gripped me, a compulsion so deep that I would have to withdraw from another project I was in. I knew I would have to take the journey with David Young, Glenn Gould, Richard Rose, Bach and ... yes, I was almost going to say God ... and yes that is what I mean, but the word has such a clutter of associations – a bit like the bad action of a poor piano, utter misrepresentation. But I was gripped by something. To be sure, Bach was already a companion of mine, and I owed much of my musical awakening to Gould's shocking clarity of playing. But David's play was stirring something else in me.

A genius called Glenn Gould, while performing the works of Bach, Schoenberg, Beethoven and the like, had not only given voice to great music but also to the silence and space contained within it. In that interior architecture of silence lay veiled dimensions and structures which have drawn so many to the pursuit of the mystic and religious. I felt the play winding these ideas and feelings together, travelling into the wonder and enigma of great music and a great musician.

I continued reading that early draft of *Glenn*, sometimes perplexed, sometimes confused. It was not an easy read. I imagined it must be like reading a score, at times trying to carry up to four lines of music in your head ... impossible for mortals like me. Indeed the play has a musical shape, for the structure parallels the Goldberg Variations. As Bach uses up to four musical voices, David Young chose to write a quartet of characters for Gould: the Puritan, Prodigy, Perfectionist and Performer. I found as the play progressed from scene to scene – or rather from variation to variation – that the 'Goulds' related not only as characters in a drama, but also as musical voices or themes. It was not only the character narrative and interactions which propelled the play, but also how their lives played contrapuntally to one another. For as Bach explores musical counterpoint, so David Young explores character counterpoint.

And here is where we must learn from the brilliance of Gould's presence at the keyboard. Through his fingers counterpoint was less a musical tool, and more an illumination of music and space. The art of counterpoint became the articulation of the inconceivable – the awareness of structure beyond. Sit down with either of Glenn Gould's studio recordings of the Goldbergs and you will become aware of not only the perpetually evolving contrapuntal 'space' between the lines of music, but also the 'space' between his fingerings in each line. Even in passages of great speed there is an impossible evocation of tangible air.

This seems to me to be the directorial challenge in this play. The physical counterpoint through blocking or what-have-you must underscore and illuminate the play of characters above it. This is one of Gould's sources of clarity and I think it must also exist in the playing of this play. The linear dramatic threads of the play are there, but the deeper 'structural' relations between characters, found in the counterpoint, also propel the play.

The acting challenge of the piece is not only whether the cast should attempt impressions of Glenn Gould – I personally think it's more of a case of intimation than imitation – but also how the characters of the Puritan, Prodigy, Perfectionist and Performer play independently, yet are utterly entwined. Usually as an actor one takes responsibility for a single character, an aspect of a scene's dynamic, one thread in the overall structure of the play. In *Glenn* I think the actor's responsibility is broader. You *are* all four 'characters' and yet you play only one. So the more each Glenn can hear and understand the musical lines of his three brothers, the more informed his performance will be. This is an enormous amount of extra work but the richness in this play parallels the richness of Gould's work at the keyboard. There must be unheard dialogue between the 'Goulds', much as there is an unheard dialogue between the musical voices in the Goldberg Variations. This is new dramatic territory, but the play itself is new dramatic territory.

The ground of the play also bears humour, mischief, whimsy, farce and vaudeville, all spun through the prism of Gould. I encourage you to expect no more from the play's culmination than you might from the culmination of the Goldbergs themselves – a path through time, accompanied by a meditation of theme and variation which, by the final aria, gives the illusion of returning to the beginning. The pilgrim may leave the great cathedral by the path he entered, but his soul has been given new breath. It has rested momentarily outside of time in the presence of mystery and elation. A cathedral is a structure which can wake us from the anaesthetic of the everyday. So it is with Bach's Goldberg Variations. And so it is with David Young's *Glenn*.

While I feel there is no centrepiece to the play as such, for me the 25th Variation is the 'ganglia' that permeates the entire structure. Here the play enters a peculiarly arrested period of loss and longing, a deeply etched ache of being separate, the solitary sadness that was much of Gould's own path. The sweet ache, the pain of separateness informs much of Gould's song, that strange, embarrassing half-singing which is still to be heard in the background of his recordings.

Don't be alarmed if, at the conclusion of the play, the person of Glenn remains an enigma. Where and how he heard those strains of music, how he articulated silence itself, how he lived 'between the notes' of the everyday world, how he accessed the rapturous place he often entered while playing, these are the mysteries suspended in the half-light of Gould's cathedral and in David Young's play.

– R.H. Thomson

Production History

Glenn was first produced by the Necessary Angel Theatre Company at the duMaurier Theatre Centre in Toronto, September 1992.

Directed by Richard Rose
Dramaturgy by Paul Ledoux and Don Kugler
Musical Direction by Don Horsburgh
Set and Lighting Design by Graeme S. Thomson
Costume Design by Charlotte Dean
Choreography by Susan McKenzie
Sound Design by Richard Mendonca
Stage Managed by Debra McKay
          assisted by Cara Millson

Cast
The Prodigy, Duncan Ollerenshaw
The Performer, Randy Hughson
The Perfectionist, Henry Czerny
The Puritan, R.H. Thomson

Playwright's Note

This is a difficult play to convey in book form because the time-space conventions of naturalistic theatre are put to strange tests on almost every page. The central conceit is that we are inside Glenn Gould's head, and that anything is possible. Each character can invoke time-space shifts, or be subjected to time-space shifts invoked by others. A few clarifying comments to ease the reader's journey:

The Goldberg Variations: Gould began and ended his recording career with Bach's Goldberg Variations. The play follows the voicing, structure and mood of Bach's score. For example, if a variation is an arabesque with two voices, there are two characters in the scene; if the variation is a canon then the two characters play a game of chase. The notion of contrapuntal voicing, and parallel action, is central to the dramatic structure throughout. The goal is harmonic, rather than melodic unity. The 'ground bass' mentioned in the stage directions refers to the thirty-two-note progression established in the opening aria.

Each variation features recorded music culled from Glenn Gould's life in the studio. His early and late recordings of the Goldberg Variations receive prominent coverage, but the score draws liberally from his entire *oeuvre*. In some cases the recorded material is sampled with computer technology – a musical phrase looped, phased, compressed or elongated to highlight some aspect of Gould's technique or the harmonic dimensions of the music itself.

At no time does an actor sit at the keyboard and pretend to play one of Glenn Gould's recorded performances.

Entrances and Exits: In most cases entrances and exits indicated in the stage directions refer to characters entering and leaving lit playing areas. The characters rarely leave the stage entirely.

Furniture and Props: There are a number of chairs on stage: Gould's famous piano chair, a swivel chair in the recording studio, a plain chair which serves multiple functions and a recliner at the family cottage in Uptergrove. At a couple of key moments a hanging piano harp drops into the action from above. There is a recording console with a telephone. All other props are carried on and off by the cast. Less is more.

Other Dramatis Personae: 'Jessie' refers to Jessie Grieg, Glenn Gould's cousin and lifelong soul-mate. Jessie never appears onstage in person.

From time to time the four characters assume the guise of the alter egos Glenn Gould developed in his humourous writings *viz.* Theodore Slutz and Wolfgang von Krankmeister. At other times they play real people like Herbert von Karajan, or invented characters like Mr Ramsay or Larry Lewman. The convention here is one of gamesmanship and blatant role-playing. At no time does the audience lose sight of the Gould-behind-the-mask.

At its premiere in Toronto the play was performed in the round.

May 14, 1999

Act One

[*Music under: Seigfried Idyll. Lights fade. As the lights come down we listen to a tape collage of on-the-street interviews with representatives from a range of age groups and ethnic backgrounds.*]

VOICES: [*a building crescendo*] ... a famous pianist ... dunked his hands in this really hot ... hat, scarf, gloves – does that count for three? ... quit performing ... child prodigy ... I think he was part lizard ... total hypochondriac ... swear you were looking at the young Bob Dylan ... a hermit ... from the Beaches ... this special stool ... photographic memory ... night owl ... the guy sneezes on the phone and Gould ... a monk ... the singing ... obsessed with technology ... drove around all night... he took pills ... Fran's Restaurant ... pretty sure he was ... a recluse ... gay? ... a piano player, right? ... a telephone addict ... hated the cold ... loved the north ... the Goldbergs ... wasn't he Jewish? ... lived on scrambled eggs ... this thing about solitude ... listen, I'm going to have to call you right back. I've got Glenn Gould on the other line – that's right, Glenn Gould!

[*The tape reaches peak volume, stops abruptly. To black. A single piano note sounds – the first note of the ground bass from the Goldberg Variations. The note reverberates, fades down to silence.*]

Aria

[*Music up: Aria, early version. Lights up on the four Glenns dressed in overcoats, hats, scarves and gloves appear from the shadows. They move in unison out of the semi-darkness, each performing a personal vocabulary of gestures, conducting the inner music of self. At the end of the Aria, lights shift. Another note from the ground bass.*]

Variation 1: Ecstasy

[*The Puritan moves toward the audience. The Prodigy goes to a table, picks up a yellow, legal-length pad and begins to write. Music up: Variation 1, late version.*]

PURITAN: I recently re-recorded the Goldberg Variations, returning to Bach's text in my forty-eighth year. As a prelude to the recording sessions I of course felt obliged to listen to my original interpretation of the score which is now some thirty-one years old ...

[*Cross-fade to Variation 1, early version. Light on: the Prodigy reads from his yellow legal-length pad. The Puritan is turned away from him. They remain unaware of one another.*]

PRODIGY: Letter to posterity. I am about to record the Goldberg Variations. I spent this morning going over the score and for the first time I could hear the entire thing in my head.

PURITAN & PRODIGY: [*in unison*] It was a spooky experience.

[*They are both startled by the echo effect. They still can't see each other.*]

PRODIGY: I felt as if I was standing outside myself, listening with my inner ear to music I was born to play ...

PURITAN: My first impression was that there was quite a bit of piano playing on that record, and I mean that in the most derogatory sense possible. Strangely, I could not recognize or identify with the *spirit* of the person who made that recording.

PRODIGY: I felt like I was listening to someone else ... And the music he was playing! I was ... transported!

[*He begins to move in a rhapsodic dance.*]

PURITAN: The condition of ecstasy is a kind of standing apart from the self. I have spent my life trying to sustain that moment of rapturous transcendence.

PRODIGY: The music carrying me up and up and up!

PURITAN: When the world is young ecstasy is a kind of sensual drunkenness. You rush around after it, exhilarated by the happy accidents and disorders of intuition.

[*Cross-fade to Variation 1, late version.*]

PURITAN: Years of sober reflection bring a deeper understanding and the ecstasy of youth becomes yet another thing to be transcended –

PRODIGY: When did all of this begin? Those Sunday afternoon drives home from Lake Simcoe when I first learned to listen ...

PURITAN: In maturity, ecstasy becomes a kind of ... inconsolable longing.

PRODIGY: Grey light fading into grey land. February in Ontario. Bare trees in patches. A farm house with one light on, the pond scraped clean where kids were skating.

[*Cross-fade to Variation 1, early version.*]

PURITAN: One longs to be part of some larger unity. The moment bursting open. 'All the bells that ever rung still ringing in the long, dying light.'

PRODIGY: Mother tunes in the New York Philharmonic on the CBC. The music swells to fill the car ... rings harmonics in my inner ear ... The music coming to life inside my head! Unity! Coherence! Structure! Me playing it all!

[*He conducts the music he's hearing in his head.*]

PURITAN: I sense that I am entering a period of great change ... as I cross this threshold into the unknown I must remember everything I ever knew about bravery ... in such moments, one cocks an ear toward the past ... one *listens*.

PRODIGY: I am Busoni! And Bach never sounded so good!

[*The Puritan and the Prodigy exit without connecting. The Perfectionist moves from behind his console. Light shift. Another note from the ground bass.*]

Variation 2: The Ivory Tower

[*The Perfectionist cues the engineer. The red light bulb which stands in for the camera blinks on. The Perfectionist addresses it as he moves around the console.*]

PERFECTIONIST: Take-twoness. If you don't understand the concept of take-twoness you'll never understand me. I mean, really, who is to say that on *this* night at *this particular* piano we are going to hear *this* performer's definitive rendering of the work in question? The odds are against it, so I moved on. It's here in the studio, with the technical potential offered by many takes, many discrete creative decisions, where the artist can truly make works of transcendental significance ...

[*He sits down in a swivel chair in front of the 'camera'.*]

Embracing that recognition, I withdrew from the concert stage some fifteen years ago and began to make controversial public pronouncements about the future of serious music. Not surprisingly, the critics came after me with pitches and torchforks. Stop tape. Drat!

[*He pats his face dry with a handkerchief. The red light blinks off. The Prodigy rushes out and pours a bag of dominoes on the stage. The Puritan enters talking on the telephone. Music up: scoring based on Variation 2. As the Prodigy counts out his dominoes he sings the notes of the bass line.*]

PRODIGY: [*under other dialogue*] One, two, three, four, five, six, seven, eight, nine, ten, eleven, twelve, thirteen, fourteen, fifteen, sixteen, seventeen, eighteen, nineteen, twenty, twenty-one, twenty-two, twenty-three, twenty-four, twenty-five, twenty-six, twenty-seven, twenty-eight, twenty-nine, thirty, thirty-one, thirty-two.

PURITAN: Just a minute, Susan, Jessie has arrived [*light cue*], yes, my cousin Jessie, and I want her to … repeat that last part. [*to Jessie*] *The New York Times* review.

[*The Prodigy finishes counting out the dominoes, pulls out a bag of candy Love Hearts and shakes one loose. He reads the phrase written on it.*]

PRODIGY: 'Luv U 4 Ever.'

[*He thinks about eating it, then puts it away.*]

PURITAN: 'The new Goldbergs are less viscerally intoxicating … but more affecting. More *serious*. More seductive in their depth …' [*to Jessie*] Who should be hearing this right now, Jessie?

PRODIGY: Mother!

[*He begins putting dominoes on end in a large arc, counting as he goes.*] [*under*] Aria, one. Two. One, two, three.

[*The Perfectionist cues the engineer. The red light comes back on and he re-addresses himself to it.*]

PERFECTIONIST: [*adjusting his posture*] How was I? Like this? Not surprisingly, the critics came after me with torches and pitchforks. Fine. Let's move on. [*host mode*] Torches and pitchforks. Criticism and Labels. Early on in my performing career I discovered that the gladiatorial element inherent in the concert situation encouraged the worst tendencies in the musical press. 'Mr Gould waving to and fro on his pygmy piano stool affects strange mannerisms ...'

PURITAN: [*into phone*] What was that last bit? [*repeating to Jessie*] 'The contemplative meditation of the Aria, the splendid varieties of attack in the 15th Variation ...' [*cupping the receiver*] It gets better, Jessie.

PERFECTIONIST: Instead of entering into the rapturous state of *innerness* which *real listening* engenders the critics kept their eyes wide open and saw a man in ill-fitting evening wear conducting himself at the keyboard. One might have expected that after I retired from the 'pro tour' the critics would have found something else to talk about.

PRODIGY: [*structuring his dominoes*] One, two, three. One, two, three. One, two, three. One.

PURITAN: [*relaying to Jessie*] '... the detached and crystalline character of the epic 25th ... the almost frightening clarity in the virtuosic parts ...'

PERFECTIONIST: No such luck. 'In his most recent recordings of Mozart, Mr Gould continues to show an unrepentant desire to shock the grown-ups.'

PRODIGY: Mother!

PERFECTIONIST: Well, let me assure you, by now I've read *all* the labels.

PURITAN: [*relaying to Jessie*] '... create a Goldberg that gives both a sense of ecstasy ... and of quiet repose.' And who should be hearing this?

PRODIGY: Mother!

PERFECTIONIST: 'Gould the Recluse.'

PURITAN: Susan, thanks so much for calling this in. Yes. Indeed. Perhaps someday soon we'll have an opportunity to meet face to face [*he hangs up*] – or not. Well, Jessie, for once, a critic understood, but I'm not about to take it deeply to heart.

PERFECTIONIST: 'Gould the Neurotic Wreck.'

PURITAN: Sunday painters believe their reviews.

PRODIGY: [*under*] Mother! Two, three. One, two, three. One, two, three. One. Two. Three. One. Two-two. Three. Aria.

PERFECTIONIST: 'Gould the Stoic.'

PURITAN: It's a bit late in the day for the musical press to be doing me any favours.

PERFECTIONIST: 'Gould the Sexual Enigma.'

[*The Prodigy contemplates the avenue of dominoes he has assembled.*]

PRODIGY: So *beautiful*.

PURITAN: Jessie, I know the story they want to tell:

PRODIGY: [*points at first domino*] Aria.

PURITAN: The eccentric piano virtuoso, now paunchy and grey of skin, goes back to re-record the work that established him as a young artist. The theme-and-variation of the music a template for the arc of the performer's life – the melodic figurations of early genius transformed by the burdens of age –

PRODIGY: [*points at seventeenth domino*] French Overture.

PURITAN: ... all of it supposedly there in Bach's text.

PRODIGY: The 25th Variation.

PERFECTIONIST: 'Gould the Vaudevillian.'

PURITAN: I can hear Herr von Hockmeister now: [*German accent*] 'Dis is all part of Mr Gould's continuing quest for autobiographical martyrdom.'

PERFECTIONIST: 'Gould the Technological Quack.'

PRODIGY: [*points at second last domino*] Quodlibet. Latin for 'as you like it'.

PURITAN: Pardon?

PERFECTIONIST: 'Gould the Pharmaceutical Enthusiast.'

[*The Prodigy fishes another candy love heart out of the bag, reads it, then pops it in his mouth.*]

PRODIGY: 'You R the 1.' [*points at last domino*] Aria.

> [*A beeper goes off on the Puritan's watch. He pushes a button to silence it. Retrieves a vial of pills from his coat pocket, shakes one loose and swallows it. Takes his own pulse. All of this is very routine.*]

PERFECTIONIST: 'Gould the Hypochondriac.'

> [*The Prodigy sings the notes of the bass line, very fast.*]

PURITAN: I am taking care of myself, Jessie. I've been working eighteen hours a day. I should look even worse.

PRODIGY: [*exiting*] Mother! I've figured out the Goldbergs!

PERFECTIONIST: The funny thing about this proliferation of labels is that none of them properly identifies the real Glenn Gould.

PURITAN: I know you're worried, Jessie. So am I. I've always *been* worried.

> [*He looks at his hands for a long moment.*]

All of this is borrowed.

> [*He turns away from Jessie's chair. Light shift to dappled shadow. Sound cue: Arctic wind. The Puritan moves the length of the stage and bends to study the dominoes the Prodigy left onstage. Lights fade. Another note from the ground bass.*]

Variation 3: The Polar Sea versus Red

> [*Cross-fade to sounds of an orchestra tuning up. The Performer paces on stage. He's wound very tight. He takes his own pulse. The Puritan moves in his own distance, observing. He is invisible to the other players.*]

PERFORMER: Borderline arrhythmia.

> [*He takes a pill. The Puritan finishes collecting the dominoes. The Performer paces and conducts himself, trying to concentrate on the unheard music. The Perfectionist sneaks up behind him, blindfolds him with his hands.*]

PERFECTIONIST: Ready to play?

PERFORMER: No. But nevertheless, I will be playing, in about five minutes.

PERFECTIONIST: I mean, the game.

PERFORMER: You never get tired of it, do you?

PERFECTIONIST: Fish swim. Birds fly. I play the game. And this is a canon.

PERFORMER: [*sardonic*] Well then, I suppose I could give you a run.

PERFECTIONIST: I was thinking more along the lines of a lightening fast encirclement.

PERFORMER: Ho-ho, aren't we robust this evening –

PERFECTIONIST: Indeed. Got someone in mind?

PERFORMER: I don't know. Let me see …

> [*He turns in a slow, deliberate circle, conducting with little gestures of one hand. He holds finger to temple.*]

PERFECTIONIST: You always do that when you're trying to know.

PERFORMER: I don't *try to* know, my friend. I *know*.

> [*The Prodigy enters in a foul mood.*]

PRODIGY: *Mother* thinks she knows and she doesn't, Jessie. That's the problem. When I say I know, I *know*. When she says she knows she only *thinks* she knows.

PERFORMER: [*throwing down the gauntlet.*] Okay. I've got someone. Go ahead.

PERFECTIONIST: Someone I know?

PRODIGY: Have you listened to the way she talks? There should be a roadside shrine!

> [*The Puritan homes in on the Prodigy. The Prodigy is unaware of his presence.*]

PERFORMER: Someone you know and would like to know better.

PRODIGY: [*parroting his mother*] I always wanted a classical pianist. I played music all the time I was carrying him and prayed for a gift from God.

PERFECTIONIST: Hm.

PRODIGY: [*mother's voice*] He'd sit on my knee at the piano and hit a single note with one finger. Then he'd listen until the sound had entirely faded away ... *fish wrap.*

[*He resumes his writing. The Puritan reads over his shoulder.*]

She makes me see red, Jessie. And that's *dangerous.*

PERFECTIONIST: This person you're thinking of – if she were a body of water which body of water would she be?

PERFORMER: Did I say this person was a 'she'?

PERFECTIONIST: Water is always feminine.

PRODIGY: [*reading to Jessie*] Special to *The Daily Woof*. 'Mozart Sez: Fungus Amungus!'

[*He goes back to writing.*]

PERFORMER: I'd be the Polar Sea.

[*The words 'polar sea' spark the Puritan's interest. He approaches the Performer and the Perfectionist.*]

PERFECTIONIST: Aha. The feminine principle embedded in a barren landscape. Interesting paradox.

[*A piano chord sounds. The Puritan feels a sting of pain, looks up, seeking the source.*]

PRODIGY: [*calling out*] G-diminished-seventh ... mother! [*reading to Jessie*] 'Mozart the budgie has come down with an under-feather fungus. According to the budgie: [*Mozart voice*] Glenn and his mother can't decide who is da boss ...'

[*Another chord sounds. More pain for the Puritan.*]

E! A! B-flat! C! F! Major and minor seconds sandwiched between perfect fourths! I'm not slouching! [*reading, Mozart voice*] 'Das Vunder Kind is currently banished to his room and forbidden to touch da piano until further notice' – who cares about stupid report cards?

PERFECTIONIST: Would you more often be stormy or calm?

PERFORMER: Given the right conditions I can be very, very stormy. And when I'm stormy, watch out.

PRODIGY: [*as he writes*] I'm serious, Jessie, I could kill her.

PERFECTIONIST: Hostile!

PERFORMER: Remote, not hostile.

PRODIGY: [*interrupting her*] Jessie, I *see* red, but I'm not temperamentally inclined to *act* red.

[*He continues his writing.*]

PERFECTIONIST: Most people think of the Polar Sea as hostile.

PERFORMER: The Polar Sea is a paradox – frozen, yet *brimming* with life. To stand in her presence is to become a philosopher.

PRODIGY: I'm a prisoner, Jessie ...

[*The word 'prisoner' sparks the Puritan's interest. He returns his attention to the Prodigy.*]

PERFECTIONIST: An explorer in the thrall of the Great Unknown?

PERFORMER: In seeking truth we become part of the truth we seek. That is an official clue.

PERFECTIONIST: The anthropic principle?

PERFORMER: Precisely. The human mind cannot escape the net of its own thinking.

[*Another chord. Another shot of pain for the Puritan.*]

PRODIGY: [*to mother*] G! C-sharp! D! G-sharp! The intervalus diabolus, two of them! Separated by a minor second! [*to Jessie*] I *hate* this stupid game.

PERFECTIONIST: Werner Heisenberg.

PERFORMER: Wrong side of the brain.

PRODIGY: I've got to escape.

[*The Puritan is close to the Prodigy now, hanging on his every word.*]

PERFECTIONIST: I'm in a box canyon here.

PRODIGY: I'm going to chart my own course.

PERFORMER: Think 'horizon line'. When you look into my eyes you feel like you can see forever.

PERFECTIONIST: Barbra Streisand!

PERFORMER: Wrong side of the galaxy. Imagine an outpouring of emotion that's cool to the touch.

PRODIGY: [*holding up his two hands*] *This* is all I own, Jessie. I can't expect others to understand. [*deep breath*] Every escape begins with ... one ... small ... step.

[*He stands, hesitates, looking off toward his mother.*]

PERFECTIONIST: I'm going nowhere!

PRODIGY: Mother? I *apologize*, okay?

[*He exits.*]

PERFECTIONIST: Pardon my moment of pique. Lets try another tack. If this person were a chair, what kind of chair would he be?

PERFORMER: Are chairs male?

PERFECTIONIST: Usually.

PERFORMER: I'd be ... an uncomfortable throne.

[*The Puritan slowly sits down on the chair. Lights fade. Another note from the ground bass.*]

Variation 4: Creative Deception

[*The Puritan sits alone on his uncomfortable throne. The Perfectionist enters and sits in front of the camera. The Puritan watches him closely. The Perfectionist is unaware of the Puritan.*]

PURITAN: Studio G in the CBC building on Jarvis Street – my beautiful prison. I spent thousands of hours in this room fabricating a certain kind of truth. I ruled here like a Roman emperor, building great aqueducts for the sound of myself.

[*The Perfectionist cues his engineer. The red camera light blinks on.*]

PERFECTIONIST: [*to camera*] To grasp the biographer's art one must first understand how disparate eras cohere, and that means understanding the splice.

PURITAN: [*refuting him*] Most biographers are forgers, forever trying to situate their heroes slightly in advance of the nearest historically significant movement.

PERFECTIONIST: Take Manhattan and put it alongside your mother's living room in the Beaches.

PURITAN: Glenn Gould, Canadian prodigy, is discovered in New York City and catapulted to worldwide fame. It's too easy!

PERFECTIONIST: With a single jump-cut the biographer spans a decade.

PURITAN: And misses the truth.

PERFECTIONIST: Let's have a little fun. What we're after here is the contrapuntal relationship between psyche and era. A new way to eavesdrop on the self ...

PURITAN: The process of *becoming* within the individual psyche is unconscious, indeterminate and wholly subliminal – each *day* a new era.

[*The Perfectionist is on his feet, moved by the energy of his own story.*]

PERFECTIONIST: First splice. Midtown Manhattan, 1955.

[*He pushes a button. Sound track: big city ambience, traffic, horns etc. The Prodigy enters wearing overcoat, cap, muffler and gloves.*]

PRODIGY: Taxi!

[*He gets into a cab.*]

PERFECTIONIST: My first impression was that New Yorkers were larger than life – flamboyant, exuberant!

PRODIGY: Columbia Masterworks, two-hundred-and-seven East Thirty Street. [*leaning forward to answer a question*] Toronto, actually. That's in Canada. Everybody up there dresses like this in June.

PERFECTIONIST: There was this one fellow, Larry Lewman. Larry was a techie in the Columbia Masterworks Studio on 30th ... this kind of guy ...

[*He physicalizes into a New York slouch.*]

PURITAN: And so the creative deception begins ...

PERFECTIONIST: [*as Larry Lewman*] I worked with all the greats over the years, Horowitz, Schnabel, Cassals – I mean, I *know* classical musicians are quirky types – but nothing prepared me for this kid. He's from Canader, right? He arrives midtown with our address on a matchbook cover and ten bucks in his pocket. The ten spot's got a moose where George Washington's supposed to be. Anyway, he arrives an hour late for the session. [*out of character*] In fact, I think I was an hour early.

PURITAN: He's wrong. I was an hour late. I'd been walking the streets alone, summoning my courage, intensely aware that one era of my life was about to end so another could begin.

> [*The Prodigy enters the recording studio and begins to lay out his supplies on a low table – Poland water, a pile of manuscripts, a tackle box full of vitamins.*]

LARRY: He saunters into the studio, it's eighty-five degrees, for crissakes, and he's dressed for a blizzard! The next thing he starts in with this kooky chair – it's a bridge chair, basically, which his dad made for him up in Canader. Collapsible. Screw fittings on the legs. Weird. He works on it – Minnesota Fats assembling a cue.

> [*The Prodigy realizes his chair is slightly off-balance. He stands and makes minor adjustments.*]

Then he asks for a basin of hot water, make it scalding he says. The kid rolls up his sleeves and puts his arms in up to here.

PRODIGY: Anybody else find it a little cool in here?

> [*He soaks his arms.*]

LARRY: It's a stinking hot June day, he's got his arms in boiling water and he's asking us to turn off the air conditioning!

PRODIGY: [*proud smile*] I have borderline tracheitis.

LARRY: So we're thinking, o-o, call Bellevue, but then he sits down at the piano ...

[*The Prodigy moves toward the keyboard, raises his hands to play. Snap to black. We listen in the dark while Glenn Gould plays a blindingly brilliant passage. Lights up: the Performer gets up from the piano very slowly, coming back to himself by degrees.*]

PERFORMER: Or something like that –

LARRY: It was like he was on bennies! Then he turns to the 25th Variation – and he crawls through it. I mean, I had to ask him: [*to the Performer*] The 25th Variation, kid. The tempo. What gives?

PERFORMER: Everything generates out of the aria – the ground bass line is duplicated and reduplicated in the variations.

LARRY: Hey, I know the score!

[*He sings the first notes of the bass line.*]

What's that got to do with the tempo in the 25th?

PERFORMER: Think architecture. The Aria and the first two Variations at the beginning. The Quodlibet and the Aria at the end. Framed between these two support structures, variations are grouped in threes. First, a canon: intense contrapuntal games, question and answer, theme chasing theme. Second: An independent variation darting this way and that like a hummingbird. And, last but not least, the sinuous dance of a two-manual arabesque. And there's your structure.

LARRY: But the 25th – so help me God, you *crawled* through it!

PERFORMER: You're not inside it yet. Nine of these three-variation units grouped like the columns in a baroque church. One in three and three in one. Does that suggest anything to you?

LARRY: A club sandwich?

PERFORMER: The Holy Trinity embedded in a sacred architecture of sound! Pattern and control in the service of spiritual ecstasy, that's the *essence* of Bach!

LARRY: You're a beat poet. Go daddy-o!

PERFORMER: The sublime paradox is that the physical reality of this music has, what?, a momentary existence in the mind of the listener. It's a pulse of intense feeling that illuminates the means of its own transmission. The sacred.

LARRY: Amen. Now, why was the 25th so slow?

PERFORMER: What has gone before? A processional of songs, dances, declamations and meditations has carried us deep inside Bach's cathedral. Now, with the 25th, we are granted a pause, an opportunity to cast our eyes up to the rose window and meditate upon the larger mysteries. There's no such thing as 'going too slow' in a moment like that.

LARRY: Ok, I buy it, but –

PERFORMER: [*interrupting*] Wait, my friend, this is a spiritual journey. [*New York accent*] 'It ain't over 'till it's over'. Five more Variations and then the Aria repeats – a suggestion of perpetuity. There's a sense that this music has neither end nor beginning, neither climax nor resolution. The composition, like Baudelaire's lovers –

PURITAN & PERFORMER: '... rests lightly on the wings of the unchecked wind.'

> [*The Performer double-takes. The Perfectionist is shaken. The Puritan approaches the scene with new interest, moving close to the Performer.*]

PERFORMER: We are looking at nothing less than the marriage of music, mathematics and metaphysics ... at transcendence itself. Don't we all want to defy death?

PERFECTIONIST: Stop tape. [*stepping out of the moment*] He's too young to know anything about death.

> [*The Puritan 'conducts the moment'.*]

PERFORMER: It's in this room with us – one breath away.

[*The Puritan is startled. He looks at his hands with great sadness.*]

LARRY: You're a looney-tune, kid. I like that. You're gonna love living down here.

PERFORMER: Live here? No thanks. I prefer Lake Simcoe.

LARRY: Lake Simcoe?

PERFORMER: The Canadian out-back. The wild frontier. That's my home.

[*Larry does a take on that.*]

LARRY: You're pulling my leg.

PERFORMER: Quite the contrary, I can walk out the back door of my cabin and go two thousand miles straight north without encountering another human being. Growing up alongside that fact does something to the architecture of thought itself. Bach would have loved the high Arctic.

LARRY: I'd be scared shitless.

[*The Performer is at a loss for words.*]

PURITAN: You'd be less certain of your importance.

LARRY: What you want to bet you'll end up in Manhattan?

PERFORMER: I'll bet you ... my life.

[*Lights fade. Another note from the ground bass.*]

Variation 5: Fish and Fisherman

[*Sound: bird calls. The single piercing note of a cardinal. The Prodigy enters carrying a fishing rod. The Puritan moves quickly offstage to retrieve a rod of his own.*]

PRODIGY: My mother and father worry that somehow the world will steal my childhood. That's why dad bought this cottage up on Lake Simcoe. It's my refuge. A place for me to connect with the important stuff ... trees ... birds ... bass fishing. Even here in paradise I am aware of a degree of separation. Others don't feel what I am feeling, [*stepping into the boat*] take Mr Ramsay, our neighbour. Mr Ramsay is a simple man with a narrow range of emotional responses.

PURITAN: [*as Mr Ramsay*] Keep the tip moving, Professor. Gotta keep it moving. That's it. You want to fool that fish. Are you on bottom? You're not fishing if you're on bottom. [*he intercedes with the Prodigy's fishing technique*] You want the fish to think the worm is alive.

PRODIGY: Mr Ramsay has taken it upon himself to provide me with some of the trappings of a normal childhood. The dog paddle. The sheep shank. The dramaturgy of worms.

[*His fishing rod quivers.*]

[*whisper*] Oh no. Think I got a nibble.

MR RAMSAY: [*whisper*] He's gumming it. Don't move.

PRODIGY: Mr Ramsay and I play our little game. He puts a worm on my hook. I play out my line until I feel the worm settle on bottom. I don't want to fool the fish. I want to fool Mr Ramsay.

[*He jerks his line.*]

I stare at the distant shore and *listen* ...

[*Mr Ramsay turns to listen, momentarily out of character as he eavesdrops on the boy.*]

I'm inside Bach's music so much of the time now. I open a new score and the possibilities flash by me like dazzling lures – *Zing! Zing!*

[*Mr Ramsay casts with a loud zing, and continues eavesdropping.*]

I turn each new piece of music around in my head for days, structure moving like the shapes of a mobile as I assemble the mental image ... this emotion against that tempo! This wind against that light! The symmetries ring in the deep place between the notes. [*in wonder*] I converse

with the dead. A joyous whispering of secrets. [*pause*] I
want to be the greatest interpreter of Bach since Busoni.

> [*Sound: the call of a cardinal. The twang of a breaking piano string.
> The beep of a life support system. Light shift: to red. The Prodigy's rod
> bends double, line races off his reel.*]

Something is happening!

MR RAMSAY: My goodness! Oh my goodness! Reel in! No!
The other way! Look out, he's running! Let the drag off!
THE DRAG!

PRODIGY: [*overlapping with Ramsay*] Stop! Just do – any! – stop!
It's-it's wrong! I-I won't be part of it!

> [*Pandemonium as the fish breaks water in a blaze of light and sound,
> then lands on the floorboards of the boat between them. Sound: fish
> thumping against boat. The Puritan goes into a horrified freeze. The
> Prodigy steps away from the boat, trying to escape.*]

The fish explodes from the water and lands in our boat. I
see everything from the fish's point of view – its entire
being this single glittering muscle. It flops on the floor
boards – a fast cadence changing time in sporadic shud-
ders ... the fish drowning in my air ... the movement
becomes legato, soft little thumps ... as the sparkle dulls
... fades ... disappears. Dead eyes. Scales gone white.
Silence ...

PURITAN: ... and me screaming at the top of my lungs.

> [*Lights fade. Another note from the ground bass.*]

Variation 6: Turning Away

[*Music up: Scriabin. The Performer and the Perfectionist enter. The Prodigy stands off to one side, facing away from them, still recovering from the horror of his fishing expedition.*]

PERFECTIONIST: The uncomfortable throne, the hostile ocean that brims with life, the mind caught in the net of its own thinking – I have another line of questioning.

PERFORMER: Play ball.

[*The Puritan enters carrying a baseball and glove. He is still shaken by events in the previous variation. He moves toward the Prodigy, looking for an opening. The Perfectionist and the Performer carry on unaware.*]

PERFECTIONIST: If this person ran for office.

PERFORMER: Sorry, I don't run. It's against my nature.

PERFECTIONIST: Not a political bone in your body?

PERFORMER: Indirect questions only, please.

[*The Puritan thwacks ball into glove. The Prodigy turns, sees the Puritan for the first time.*]

PURITAN: [*as Larry*] You're Glenn Gould, the piano player.

PRODIGY: I am. And who are you?

LARRY: Larry. I coach little league over at the park. The Cardinals. The lads talk about you.

PRODIGY: I'll bet they do.

PERFECTIONIST: Let me put it this way then, if I were a political figure with whom our mystery guest *identified* … ?

LARRY: It must be pretty rough.

PRODIGY: What do you mean?

PERFORMER: Okay, I'll just say it. Ghandi.

LARRY: I hear they call you 'Ears'.

PERFECTIONIST: [*thinking*] Ghandi. Ghandi. Ooo, the forkball.

PRODIGY: I-I have rather prominent ears.

PERFORMER: Think about what he lived face to face with.

LARRY: I told them you were brave. For doing what you're doing.

PERFECTIONIST: Death. Ghandi lived face to face with death.

PRODIGY: Brave people stand in front of bullets. I'm afraid that's not my style.

[*He turns away from the Puritan again. The Puritan bangs ball into mitt, waiting for another opening.*]

PERFORMER: Now examine if you will his vocabulary of responses to that situation. Good gracious, why am I giving you all these clues?

PERFECTIONIST: Your insatiable need to please. The Performer's perversity.

PERFORMER: A perversity which you have relinquished, I suppose ...

PERFECTIONIST: A perversity which I have learned to transcend ...

LARRY: Have you told your mother you're quitting school?

PRODIGY: Who said I was quitting school?

LARRY: My ... ah ... my short-stop.

PERFECTIONIST: ... let me see, Ghandi's response to death ...

[*The Prodigy turns half around.*]

PRODIGY: I-I'm thinking about it.

PERFECTIONIST: Passive resistance!

LARRY: Are you frightened?

PRODIGY: Why all these questions?

LARRY: Animal curiosity. I'd like to know ... what you know.

PRODIGY: I-I see no reason for fear.

LARRY: It's a big world out there. You only have Grade Eleven.

PRODIGY: I have ... other things.

[*He turns away again.*]

PERFECTIONIST: [*thinking*] An uncomfortable throne. A hostile ocean that brims with life. A pacifist politician.

Beware, my friend, the tumblers have begun to click ...

LARRY: But will what you have be enough?

PRODIGY: What do you mean?

LARRY: So much can happen in a life. Will what you have be
enough to sustain you over the ... the long haul?

PERFORMER: [*taunting*] Click. Click.

PRODIGY: I-I can't answer that question.

LARRY: You must.

PRODIGY: Why?

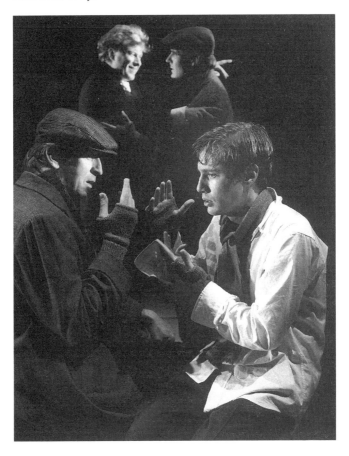

LARRY: Because ... because ... it's hard to describe – it's ...

[*He conducts himself, thinking. The Perfectionist faces the Performer with new assurance.*]

PERFECTIONIST: I *see* you. The game is the lens of my camera.

[*He and the Performer move eye to eye.*]

Click.

LARRY: [*finding the words*] – it's that you'll look back on these days for the rest of your life. You're setting a personal standard for bravery.

PRODIGY: Sir, I am not brave. I'm even afraid of that baseball ...

PERFECTIONIST: [*musing*] You're afraid of me, aren't you?

LARRY: [*extending ball and glove*] Catching it with the bare hands?

PERFORMER: Hardly ...

PRODIGY: I've never done it.

LARRY: Really, quite horrifying. I've never done it either.

PRODIGY: I thought you said you coached.

LARRY: I do. It's ... it's my way of addressing the fear.

PERFECTIONIST: Raw, animal fear. [*turning away from Performer*] You can't fool me. You have been seen.

LARRY: Want to have a go?

PRODIGY: I suppose I should be able to say I once caught a ball.

LARRY: It would be nice, just once, to throw one.

[*He winds up. Ready to throw. The Prodigy holds out his hands. Both of them are afraid. The Perfectionist wheels around.*]

PERFECTIONIST: Okay, high fast ball. Lenny Bernstein.

PERFORMER: Bernstein? Why Bernstein?

PERFECTIONIST: Lenny is a pacifist who'd never run for office. I saw him run for a cab once. Not pretty.

PERFORMER: I'm going to give you a huge clue. I want you to think about it before we play the game again.

[*The Puritan and the Prodigy are still trying to throw the ball. It's agonizing.*]

'Transcending human experience'.

[*The Puritan throws a feeble dribbler – they both turn away. The ball misses the Prodigy entirely. They turn slowly toward one another – is it over yet?*]

PERFECTIONIST: Transcending human experience ...

PRODIGY: Does that count?

LARRY: Of course it counts.

PRODIGY: Nice talking to you ...

LARRY: Where you headed?

PRODIGY: North.

LARRY: Godspeed ...

[*Lights fade. Another note from the ground bass.*]

Variation 7: Turning Toward

[*The Puritan moves around his space, picks up a yellow pad, flips through dog-eared pages covered with dense handwriting. Turns to another pad, flips its pages. Compares the two pads.*]

PURITAN: [*reading from one*] ... in this room with us, one breath away. [*reading from the other*] ... with a single splice the biographer spans a decade ... [*putting the pads aside*] One longs for clarity, for structure – the mind momentarily freed from the net of its own thinking. [*pause*] Not the midnight jottings of an insomniac.

[*The Prodigy enters, carrying a telephone, which he dials.*]

The compass needle spins in circles.

[*He sits in his chair.*]

PRODIGY: The twenty-fifth of September. No cake. No candles. No birthday celebration. Instead this ... this inconsolable longing.

[*He puts down the phone, tries to escape from its field of gravity.*]

PURITAN: There was a time when I knew how to conduct

myself in these situations. I was young, free – the world was a glorious morning spread out before me. [*spreading his arms*] I'd *run* to meet it ...

PRODIGY: [*arms spread wide*] I feel like I'm circling above my childhood, never quite finding a place to land except ...

[*He makes another move for the phone. Thwarts himself.*]

PURITAN: [*in wonder*] The *limitless* possibility of that solitary boy running into the light between the trees – [*he settles into his chair, entering the reverie*] the isolation of childhood was a doorway to ecstasy.

PRODIGY: ... except in this ... this condition of solitary confinement. The contradiction pulls at me.

PURITAN: There was a power inside *the idea* of being alone. It wasn't simply ... [*referring to himself*] a humdrum condition of life. It was a statement of *belief.*

PRODIGY: [*turning away from the phone*] I've taken myself prisoner. [*pacing again*] If I feed the doubt it will surely destroy me. I must embrace the contradiction I feel and *build* on it. But how?

[*He closes his eyes, stands poised for take-off.*]

PURITAN: That beautiful light between the trees ... banish doubt and *be there.*

[*He closes his eyes, pulls the blanket up over himself.*]

1952. Uptergrove. I told mother I wanted to see if my mechanical skills could be linked to sufficient depth of feeling – which was a nice way of saying I wanted to be utterly alone.

[*He sinks fully into his reverie, conducting himself with a finger.*]

PRODIGY: Imagine a house on stilts, the treetops are laid at my feet like a nubbly lawn. Clouds bend around the bowl of the sky. The earth is the crown of my head! [*opening his eyes*] I am atop the first tree I ever climbed. It's still my favourite. No one knows I come here. They think I'm not the tree climbing type.

[*He arrives in the uppermost branches.*]

Up as high as I can go ... on the outer edge of control –
holding tight when a sudden gust of wind snaps the
leaves around me pale green! The whole world rocks back
and forth, my heart with it!

PURITAN: Most of all, I remember it as a time when ... *I could
dream.*

[*He pulls the plaid wool throw around himself and slips into sleep.
Music sting. A burst of red light on the Prodigy. The Prodigy almost
loses his balance.*]

PRODIGY: If I fell and broke myself on the ground I would lie
down there until morning. They would never think of
looking for me here. [*pause*] There is strange beauty in that.

[*Red light shifts. Another note from the ground bass.*]

Variation 8: Pure Recognition

[*The Perfectionist addresses the red light on his camera.*]

PERFECTIONIST: Variation Eight. Take One. There are
moments in life when one understands what it is one is
really *doing.* For an instant all the clutter is swept aside
and the simple, obvious fact of your being is captured in
the mind's eye – a split-second of pure recognition. I
experienced one such moment early on in my career on
the occasion of a concert I did with Maestro von Karajan.
Now *there* was a transforming experience.

[*Music up: Beethoven's Third Piano Concerto. The Perfectionist stands,
moves away from camera.*]

You must understand that to me von Karajan was an
Olympian figure. Here was a living legend – a kind of God,

really. Night after night he stood at the centre of the world stage and held Beethoven's beating heart in his bare hands. Von Karajan on the podium while I played? It was beyond dream. It was a new kind of wakefulness. Let's go to the Konzertsaal ...

[*The Performer enters, charged up after a great performance.*]

... our performance has come to a happy conclusion and I am floating on air! I wander back out onstage after the audience has left, feeling the echo of the experience, the smell of the crowd still lingering in the air. And suddenly, there he is, the great man ... moving toward me from the wings. [*as von Karajan*] Mr Gould. I've been looking for you. Tonight was – *superior*.

PERFORMER: That's a great compliment, Maestro, thank you. I thought we acquitted ourselves rather well.

VON KARAJAN: No, no, an *incomparable* delight. I thank *you*. It was one of those rare nights. The conductor, soloist, players, and audience, all of us soaring up and up and up! The world momentarily *one thing*! [*pause*] I *heard* you tonight, Mr Gould. We all did.

PERFORMER: And I could feel you listening. It was *electrifying*.

VON KARAJAN: You must take that energy and give it to the world!

PERFORMER: I'd love to but ... but I'm not entirely sure the world wants it, Maestro.

VON KARAJAN: What do you mean?

PERFORMER: The audience. Sometimes – not tonight, mind you! – but *sometimes* ... sometimes I think they resent me.

VON KARAJAN: Of course. How is it possible not to have envy in the face of such a talented young man?

PERFORMER: They stop listening and start watching. I feel it on my skin.

VON KARAJAN: Some nights the audience will be a lover, another night it will be a wild, unbroken horse. It is a mental game. You assume control by being in control. You will learn there is much more to this business than the music itself.

PERFORMER: I'm not sure I can accommodate myself to that.

VON KARAJAN: I'm not talking about accommodation, Mr Gould, I'm talking about *self-control*. You must learn to control your image the same way you control your music.

PERFORMER: But –

VON KARAJAN: [*interrupting*] There is no other road for you to travel. You know, I heard Busoni at the height of his career, in 1922, just before he died ...

PERFORMER: Busoni ...

VON KARAJAN: ... that was thirty-five years ago. I have heard no one better in the intervening years, until tonight ...

PERFORMER: *Busoni.*

[*The Perfectionist picks up a vase holding a single rose.*]

VON KARAJAN: [*hands him the rose*] Smell it. Let me see your smile.

[*The Performer smells his rose and smiles.*]

[*normal voice*] Close-up. [*German accent*] Control is the balance point, Mr Gould. At the end of his career Busoni was dead-drunk onstage. It vas the only way he could manage. You, perhaps, have other choices. [*normal voice*] Extreme close-up. The split-second of pure recognition.

[*The Performer does a take on that. Lights shift. Another note from the ground bass.*]

Variation 9: The Road to Moscow

[*Sound: ethereal airport chimes. The opening notes of the ground bass.*]

FEMALE VOICE: Le vol neuf-zéro-neuf d'Aeroflot à Moscou a été retardé. Veuillez écouter pour renseignements supplémentaires.

[*The Performer enters with a suitcase, pauses as he passes the Puritan, who lounges in his chair.*]

PERFORMER: Did you happen to get that?

PURITAN: Your flight to Moscow is delayed.

[*The Performer crosses to sit on his suitcase. The Puritan gets up from his chair, slings a Brownie camera around his neck and moves toward him, stepping into character as 'the fan'.*]

[*as Fan*] I pray to God that doesn't mean you'll miss your concert.

PERFORMER: Excuse me ... do I know you?

FAN: You're Glenn Gould.

PERFORMER: I am.

[*The Puritan offers his hand. They do 'the Gould Shake', touching without touching.*]

FAN: I just flew in from Toronto. You were on the front page of *The Telly* yesterday.

PERFORMER: [*pleased*] Is that so?

FAN: [*seeing the headline*] 'Glenn Gould Soars to New Heights!'

PERFORMER: My-my ...

FAN: They went on and on about your concerts. From the sound of it the crowds have been going bananas!

PERFORMER: Overall, I'm very pleased with my performances. There have been moments of great emotional clarity. Thanks for saying hello.

[*He opens an edition of Kafka, sending what he thinks is a clear signal. The Puritan doesn't budge, cranes to catch a glimpse of the book his hero is reading.*]

FAN: I'm sorry. It just gives me chills being around you.

PERFORMER: Perhaps you're catching my cold. I haven't slept in two days from the sinus pain. And now I'm waiting to fly into a spring blizzard in Moscow.

FAN: You must be *terrified*.

PERFORMER: This passes for normalcy when you're a touring concert pianist. One learns to put up with it.

[*He goes back to his book. The Puritan holds his ground.*]

FAN: [*seeing the headline*] 'Plane Crash Claims Gould.'

PERFORMER: I beg your pardon –

FAN: [*eyes closed*] '... the crash occurred in a freak spring blizzard. According to eye witnesses the plane skidded sideways off the runway and disintegrated in an enormous fire ball. Already tributes from around the world are pouring in –'

PERFORMER: [*interrupting*] What are you talking about?

FAN: I'm sorry, Mr Gould, I have a vivid imagination, I got carried away. You're afraid of flying. I know all about that.

PERFORMER: Well, we do our best. Nice talking to you –

FAN: Funny, a man who fears flying lives on the high trapeze! That mid-air moment, Mr Gould! It's an honour to be in the presence of such bravery.

PERFORMER: I assure you I am not a brave man.

FAN: You're just being modest. If you weren't brave you would *never* get on that plane.

PERFORMER: I'm the first classical musician from North America to be invited behind the Iron Curtain. It was a great honour to be asked. I could hardly –

FAN: [*interrupting*] Ho-ho! I get the picture! You'd cancel but you *can't* –

PERFORMER: People lined up overnight for tickets.

FAN: You're at the mercy of their insatiable demands!

PERFORMER: I'm merely doing what I must do. My audience wants –

FAN: [*interrupting*] Human sacrifice!

PERFORMER: I'm afraid I don't understand the object of your enterprise here. I'm about to get on a plane and –

FAN: [*interrupting*] I want to understand what makes you tick! Your bravery – [*raising his Brownie*] I want a picture of the way you think, Mr Gould.

   [*He takes a snapshot. The Performer drops his book.*]

PERFORMER: [*flustered*] I am *not* a brave man! Do you want to know my terrible secret? Do you?

   [*The Puritan backs off a step. The Perfectionist gets up from his chair. He draws the Puritan's attention away from the Performer.*]

PERFECTIONIST: It's a canon. He's to play the game.

PURITAN: He doesn't feel like it.

PERFECTIONIST: It's a canon. He has no choice. [*to Performer*] If you were a household appliance?

PURITAN: A vacuum cleaner.

PERFECTIONIST: Hm. I immediately think 'information overload'.

PURITAN: [*sardonic*] Think aluminum cylinder full of dirt.

   [*The Perfectionist is grossed out, which pleases the Puritan – he returns his attention to the Performer.*]

[*as Fan*] Sorry – please – what *is* your secret?

PERFORMER: Fish fly. Birds swim. I give concerts. Please –

FAN: You're a phenomenon!

PERFORMER: I'm merely a musician.

FAN: But what a musician! People all over the Soviet Union are glued to their radios listening to your recording of the Goldbergs!

PERFORMER: That, sir, I can deal with. People sitting in the den munching a perogi while they listen to Bach on the radio. It's a hospitable image, scaled to the enterprise at hand –

FAN: Which is?

PERFORMER: – the solitary contemplation of the beauty imbedded in our musical literature.

FAN: Fear never enters into that equation, but onstage –

PERFORMER: I have one great fear, and that is that events beyond my control may divert me from my task. This flight qualifies as one such event.

FAN: What if it never gets any easier?

PERFORMER: If it never gets any easier I'll –

[*Ethereal airport chimes sound high overhead, notes from the ground bass.*]

FEMALE VOICE: Aeroflot vol neuf-zéro-neuf, un vol direct à Moscou, débarque maintenant au gare vingt-cinq.

PERFORMER: Zero hour.

FAN: But what if there is no end to the ... *difficulty*?

PERFORMER: When total strangers walk up to me in public presuming to know me – *that*, sir, I find difficult.

[*He stands up. The Puritan is suddenly overcome. He so much wanted this to go well.*]

FAN: I'm sorry. I meant no harm, Mr Gould. Your recording of the Goldberg Variations changed my life.

[*For an instant the Performer sees into this fan's vulnerability.*]

PERFORMER: I-I apologize for being abrupt. The last six months have made me very aware of myself in the eyes of others. The self-consciousness hasn't been useful.

[*Sound: a large audience before the lights go down. The Prodigy enters in overcoat and hat and sits in a chair on the stage apron.*]

FAN: You were born to perform. Perhaps public scrutiny is a fact you'll have to learn to live with.

PERFORMER: [*moving off*] There are no facts, my friend. We invent what we need and call it truth.

FAN: Godspeed –

[*Sound: audience murmurs settles. The Performer exits, leaving behind his copy of Kafka. The Puritan picks it up.*]

That fellow is amazing.

PERFECTIONIST: You've forgotten how it *was* for him!

[*Light shift. Another note from the ground bass. Sound: The sounds of an orchestra tuning up.*]

Variation 10: Pelted with Roses

[*Single spotlight on the keyboard. The Performer shuffles onstage in ill-fitting evening wear. The Puritan and the Prodigy applaud along with a pre-recorded ovation. The Perfectionist watches, very uncomfortable with all of this. The Performer takes bashful bows. He's enjoying the ovation. This is the Performer fully in control of the moment, relishing his off-beat power. The Puritan and the Prodigy watch from the sidelines, wanting this to go well. The Perfectionist watches from his own distance, biding his time. The Performer takes his seat at the piano. Snap to black. We listen to Variation 10, early version. Lights up: the Performer comes to his feet to acknowledge an enormous pre-recorded ovation which is echoed by the Prodigy and Puritan. The Perfectionist bides his time – everything is right on schedule. The Prodigy gives the Performer a bouquet of roses. The Performer smells the rose as the crowd stomps and whistles and shouts bravos. He smiles.*]

PERFECTIONIST: [*to the audience*] Roses! He wants ROSES!

[*The audience throws roses, which have been left on their seats with appropriate stage directions.*]

Give him roses!

[*The Perfectionist springs to life, goes to his console to push buttons and tweak knobs. As the roses rain down the ovation shifts, sampling in strange new sound elements one by one – the howling moan from 'the terraces' as a capacity football crowd in Glasgow pumps for the opening kick-off; eerie torch-lit chants from the Nuremberg Rally; the high-pitched ululation of Arab women from the Battle of Algiers – we are caught in a maelstrom of unleashed aural emotion. All of it conducted*] by the Perfectionist. The Puritan reacts to all of this with alarm – his body language expressing physical pain. The Prodigy cheers on with a growing sense of alarm. The Performer's bowing motion is contorted by the sheer weight of the audience's response as it continues to build into new levels of cacophony. The Perfectionist pushes more buttons. Lights shift to red. A sense of real danger now. The Performer is knocked down by a load of red roses that drop on him out of the sky. Fade to black over this action, as the audience sounds diminish to rhythmic clapping, and finally to silence. Another note from the ground bass.]

Variation 11: Chasing the Cadence

[*Music under: chanting Tibetan monks. The Performer is crumpled up in the fetal position under a pile of roses, the Puritan moves to his area in a rictus of referred pain. The Prodigy occupies his area, trying to pull himself back from the disturbance. The Perfectionist sits in his swivel chair – it's business as usual. Hushed tones prevail in the dialogue sequence which follows.*]

PERFORMER: [*raising an arm*] Pain … swelling … tenderness.

[*The Perfectionist wheels to his control panel. The Puritan is there waiting for him.*]

PERFECTIONIST: [*producing a vial of pills*] Butazolidin.

[*He pops a pill, hands the vial to the Puritan.*]

PURITAN: [*to Perfectionist*] Side effects: hypertension, insomnia, psychosis –

[*He takes a pill; this Perfectionist-Puritan action is repeated for each of the pharmaceuticals which follows. The Prodigy, meanwhile, is moving in his own space – blithe with naïve certainty.*]

PRODIGY: Candy Love Hearts. 'U R the 1.'

PERFORMER: [*diagnosing it*] Gouty inflammation of the joints.

PERFECTIONIST: Allopurinal.

PURITAN: Side-effects: unexplained sore throat, weakness in hands, taste perversion, impotence.

PRODIGY: Vitamin C.

PERFORMER: Crescent-like sensations in the fingers.

PERFECTIONIST: Zyloprim.

PURITAN: Side-effects: Edema, fever and tingling pain.

PRODIGY: Basin of hot water.

PERFORMER: Tightness in joints and muscles.

PERFECTIONIST: Librax.

PURITAN: Dilated pupils. Dry mouth. Confusion. Ataxia.

[*On the word 'ataxia' everyone takes their pulse.*]

PRODIGY: [*doing it*] Gotta soak.

PERFORMER: [*self-diagnosis*] Hypertension.

PERFECTIONIST: Aldomet.

PURITAN: Feelings of detachment. Depression. Mild psychosis including nightmares.

PRODIGY: Hot cocoa.

PERFORMER: Gout.

PERFECTIONIST: Inderal.

PURITAN: Inderal may decrease the effectiveness of Zyloprim.

PRODIGY: Hot tubby.

PERFORMER: Agitated depression!

PERFECTIONIST: Chlorpromazine.

PURITAN: Insomnia. Not to be taken with Inderal.

PRODIGY: Hot wax.

[*The Performer is startled back to full awareness.*]

PERFORMER: I can't sleep.

PERFECTIONIST: Nembutal.

PURITAN: Should be avoided in patients with impaired cardiovascular systems.

PRODIGY: [*exiting*] Coat, cap, scarf and gloves.

PERFORMER: No one understands!

[*He takes his pulse again.*]

High blood pressure.

PERFECTIONIST: Serpasil.

PURITAN: Mental depression. Impaired concentration. Decreased libido.

PERFORMER: I can't sleep … ringing in the ears.

PERFECTIONIST: Valium.

PURITAN: Hallucinations.

PERFORMER: Am I dying?

[*The Puritan moves to his chair.*]

PERFECTIONIST: Valium.

PURITAN: [*sitting down*] Clumsiness.

PERFECTIONIST: Valium.

PURITAN: Vertigo.

PERFECTIONIST: Valium!

PURITAN: Insomnia.

PERFECTIONIST: VALIUM!

PURITAN: RAGE!

PERFORMER: I need help.

PERFECTIONIST: [*spinning in his chair*] Valium. Valium. Valium.

> [*Light shift. Another note from the ground bass.*]

Variation 12: The Tel Aviv Piano

> [*The Prodigy practices the run up to a complicated cross-handed passage, stumbling at the same point each time. The Perfectionist comes back onstage, catching his breath as he brings his full attention to the Prodigy. The Prodigy struggles with his fingering error, increasingly frustrated. The Perfectionist cues the technician. The red light comes on. He addresses it.*]

PERFECTIONIST: I have a profound distrust of pianos. What draws me to Bach is the fact that the music *per se* transcends the whole issue of instrumentation.

> [*The Performer wheels a vacuum cleaner onstage, sneaking up on the Perfectionist.*]

Bach shunned the outward disorder of musical appliances

> [*The Performer turns on the vacuum cleaner. The Perfectionist must shout over the noise.*]

and focused inwardly on the musical image, which he heard exactly as he wanted to! There was an incident in Tel Aviv which I think admirably –

> [*The Prodigy stops playing and glares. The Perfectionist does likewise.*]

PRODIGY: Jessie! Can you turn that off? I'm trying to practice!

PERFORMER: The Tel Aviv story belongs to me.

[*The Perfectionist shuts off the vacuum cleaner.*]

PRODIGY: Thank you!

PERFECTIONIST: It's a canon. You are to play the game. If you were a bird which species would you be?

[*He conducts himself, thinking. The Prodigy begins to play again, stumbling at the cross-handed passage.*]

PERFECTIONIST: As I was saying –

PERFORMER: [*interrupting*] A dodo, dodo. Excuse me –

[*He steps in front of the Perfectionist and turns on the vacuum cleaner.*]

There was a peculiar episode in Tel Aviv which I think admirably demonstrates the point I'm trying to make about pianos.

PERFECTIONIST: If you were a four-wheeled vehicle?

PERFORMER: A Mack truck! I was on tour in Israel which, as everyone kept telling me, is a desert country and as a result seems to have bred a bizarre species of desert piano.

PRODIGY: Jessie, I'm stuck on a problem! Finish the vacuuming later, ok?

PERFECTIONIST: This will not do.

PERFORMER: I found myself forced to give a series of concerts on a very bad instrument –

PERFECTIONIST: – a monstrous pig of a piano!

PRODIGY: I can't hear myself think!

[*Vacuuming continues*]

Fine!

[*He sings to drown out the vacuum cleaner as he digs deeper into the difficult passage.*]

PERFORMER: This instrument had a terrible action, the equivalent of power steering, and it followed me along the rugged trail in its own special truck.

PERFECTIONIST: There was no special truck! If you were an animal in a zoo?

[*The Performer thinks while he vacuums. The Perfectionist moves to regain control of the story.*]

By the Tel Aviv engagement that piano was playing me!

[*The Prodigy races through the trouble spot again and again, singing the notes aloud. The Performer vacuums up the Perfectionist's leg toward his crotch, horrifying him.*]

PERFORMER: An elephant ... looking for peanuts!

[*The Perfectionist shuts off the vacuum cleaner. The Prodigy smiles and plays through the passage with ease.*]

I took a long walk along the seashore and ruminated on my predicament.

PERFECTIONIST: I *sat* on sand dunes! Play the game properly! If you were a machine in a science fiction movie?

[*Sound: the piano music comes suddenly clear, soars.*]

PERFORMER: Hm ...

PRODIGY: [*a major realization*] I short-circuited the problem!

PERFECTIONIST: I decided the only thing that could save me was to recreate the most admirable tactile circumstances I knew of.

PERFORMER: A teleporter! I mentally transported myself to Lake Simcoe, sat down in our cottage at the old stubby-legged Chickering and *played* the whole concert through in my head!

PERFECTIONIST: Right. Go on. They're all listening.

[*He exits. The Performer is momentarily nonplussed.*]

PERFORMER: Holding on desperately to the image of my performance at the Chickering I rushed to the auditorium, played the concert and for the first time on the entire tour I was absolutely *free* of commitment to that oinker of a piano! And the Beethoven that came out was really rather extraordinary.

[*He indicates his story is over.*]

PERFECTIONIST: [*on monitor*] Go on. Don't be afraid – the *whole* truth.

PERFORMER: [*wary*] After the concert I'm in my dressing room and Max Brod – who is Franz Kafka's literary executor – comes backstage with a woman who wants to meet me. She says: [*German accent*] 'Mr Gould, I haf attended three of your concerts in Israel and tonight ... in some vay ... something vas *different*. It was like your being vas not with us, you were ... *removed*.' Somehow she'd miraculously tapped into the mind-set I'd brought into the concert hall!

PERFECTIONIST: Get out the Ouija board, folks.

PERFORMER: Which made a pretty strong case for the existence of a privileged communication between live audience and performer!

PERFECTIONIST: – a doctrine I find *highly* suspect –

PERFORMER: – nevertheless , she'd put her finger *right on it*. I was spooked!

PERFECTIONIST: Until she looked me straight in the eye and, in all seriousness, said: 'It vas unquestionably ze finest *Mozart* I haf ever heard!' Of course, I'd been playing *Beethoven*!

PRODIGY: I can't hear the music! Jessie! Turn the vacuum cleaner on!

> [*The Perfectionist turns and gestures grandly. The stage is bathed in red light. The other players go into a freeze. The Perfectionist snaps his fingers. Lights up on the hanging piano. Another note from the ground bass.*]

Variation 13: Bloodsport

[*The Perfectionist gestures toward the harp of the concert grand which hangs suspended high above the stage. He addresses himself to the Performer with quiet rage.*]

PERFECTIONIST: Your problem, sir, is that you do not have normal filters for dealing with everyday situations and events. It can be dangerous out there if you're a peeled egg. The world bristles with sharp points and jagged corners. There came a time when you felt it all pushing in on you – it was the thirteenth of March ... the thirteenth of the third ... a very, very unlucky combination for you, my friend – your hotel room became ... a cage ...

[*He snaps his fingers, the Performer moves to stand beneath the hanging piano harp. The Perfectionist gestures dramatically, the piano harp drops toward the Performer, terrifying him.*]

PERFORMER: I call friends in distant cities in the middle of the night seeking comfort –

PERFECTIONIST: You became a notorious canceller. Your manager ran out of excuses.

[*He gestures toward the piano. It drops another foot toward the Performer.*]

PERFORMER: I-I tell them about the very real difficulties and dangers I face and they take that as evidence of my instability –

PERFECTIONIST: Friends talk to friends. The circle widens. Soon there is gossip between total strangers.

[*The Prodigy and the Puritan speak from the shadows.*]

PURITAN: He'd arrive in some major centre in the United States and find himself *unable* to play.

PERFORMER: It's a question of nerves!

PRODIGY: In a moment of desperation he actually claimed he had sub-clinical polio.

PERFECTIONIST: The next thing you know you walk into an orchestra rehearsal and the room falls silent ...

[*The hanging piano drops another foot.*]

PERFORMER: Whispering behind my back ...

PURITAN & PRODIGY: [*sotto voce*] Drinks Poland water. Never shakes hands. Superstitious. And the pills!

PERFORMER: I need them to sleep!

PERFECTIONIST: Columbia capitalized on the eccentricities from the outset, and early on you didn't mind the publicity. The audience, of course, just ate it up. You became another freak in the brothel of show business. Which is where our friends the critics took over ... [*commanding the hanging piano with gestures*] '... seldom has a more exquisite performance been heard, or a worse one witnessed. Gould's pygmy piano stool, his storm-tossed mane, his habit of collapse at the end of each solo line were all sheer show business –'

[*He drops the piano another foot. The Performer stands his ground.*]

PERFORMER: [*bravado*] 'His brave interpretation of the music, sheer genius.'

PRODIGY: 'It is a tragedy that Mr Gould's behaviour at the keyboard produced laughter in the audience.'

PERFORMER: I sing along because I can't help it!

PURITAN: [*looking up at the dangerous piano*] Finally, the phobias just ... took him over.

PERFECTIONIST: 'Why must he pounce upon the notes like a leopard upon its prey?'

PERFORMER: My technique is self-taught!

PRODIGY: He was incapable of taking instruction.

PERFORMER: I use the mental image!

PERFECTIONIST: 'Mr Gould seems to forget that he is on a concert platform!'

PURITAN: He could no longer be himself in public.

[*The Performer comes to his knees.*]

PERFORMER: [*imploring*] No one listens!

PERFECTIONIST: You, my friend, have the hearing problem!

[*Sound: fish sting. The piano drops toward the Performer. Snap to black. Another note from the ground bass.*]

Variation 14: He Hurt Me

[*The Perfectionist gestures to fly the piano harp back up into the hanging position. The Performer is splayed on the floor beneath it.*]

PERFECTIONIST: [*to camera*] I've always been a fanatic about pianos. My concern is not about the sound so much as the *action*. For me it's all about the draft of the keys. Tactile grab and immediacy. This is 'tactile immediacy'.

[*He hits a tuning fork. The Performer clutches his chest and begins his slow journey back to consciousness. In the speech that follows he comes unsteadily to his feet, still unseen by the Perfectionist.*]

Bearings, levers and linkages. Every one of them requires time to complete its cycle. I want no slack! Shallow draft on the keys, everything else cranked down two turns past tight. I want to feel the musculature of the music [*the Performer feels his right arm*]. I don't want to *think* about the instrument [*the Performer looks at his hands*] that's between me and my mental image of the music.

[*The Performer is on his feet now. He groans groggily. The Perfectionist swivels around, surprised.*]

PERFORMER: It's the nightmare where you come to consciousness in a circus cage surrounded by sleeping tigers. You feel your way around the perimeter, looking for a way out. There is no door ... no way out of the cage ... and then you turn ... and realize that one of the big cats is looking at you. [*he turns and looks at the Perfectionist*] It makes a little sound deep in its chest and rolls to its feet. You are out of control, in total free fall. You spot a whip and a chair in the centre of the cage. You move toward them as if you know what you're doing ...

[*The Perfectionist gestures, lights up on the hanging piano. The Performer looks up, goes into a freeze.*]

PERFECTIONIST: At the end of your ill-fated tour in 1959 you had to fly to Manhattan for a meeting with the people at Steinway about your recording schedule. Remember Jan Hubbert?

PERFORMER: The chief technician at Steinway –

PERFECTIONIST: A piano tuner elevated to a position only slightly below the master musicians whose instruments he serviced. You and Hubbert had had increasingly sharp disagreements, which you both repressed, about the regulation of pianos.

PERFORMER: [*remembering*] I wanted things done to my instrument that Hubbert simply would not do – mechanical adjustments that he felt were out of bounds.

PERFECTIONIST: Precisely. And *we* figured out a way to take advantage of it.

PERFORMER: We did?

PERFECTIONIST: Hubbert popped into your A&R man's office before he realized you were sitting there. [*as Hubbert, Dutch accent*] Hey, *Glenn*!

> [*The Performer is caught off guard by the Perfectionist's approach. The Perfectionist takes his hand and pumps it heartily.*]

PERFORMER: Hubbert. We-we were just talking about you. You see I'm planning to record the *Tempest* and I-I have some new ideas about the kind of preparation I'd like to try –

HUBBERT: [*interrupting*] 'New ideas', Mr Gould?

PERFORMER: [*momentarily flummoxed*] Yes.

HUBBERT: [*big smile*] Here's hoping it doesn't involve tightening the action.

PERFORMER: Well, as a matter of fact it does.

HUBBERT: I'm afraid I've exhausted the possibilities of that little experiment, Glenn. There's nothing out there but accidental rebounds and hiccups.

PERFORMER: Oh?

HUBBERT: I'd have thought after the public response to the

Beethoven one-ten the desire for hair-trigger action would have lost some of its allure for you.

PERFORMER: I'm afraid I don't understand –

HUBBERT: [*patting the Performer vigorously on the shoulders*] Oh, you're a wily one, Mr Gould. [*quoting review*] '... the unnecessary clutter of unwanted sounds in the allegro passages must surely be the consequence of a poorly prepared piano ...'

[*He gives the Performer a little shake by the neck.*]

You do what you do best. I'll do what I do best. We'll get along just fine.

[*The Perfectionist steps away, turns back to the Performer.*]

PERFECTIONIST: Hubbert *hurt* you.

PERFORMER: He *hurt* me.

PERFECTIONIST: The affidavit filed on your behalf in federal court charged that: [*reading the deposition*] 'Hubbert engaged in unduly strong handshakes and other demonstrative physical acts, ignoring the widespread and well-known fact that Mr Gould was a man of extreme and unusual sensitivity to physical contact.'

[*The Performer is now talking to a doctor, the Perfectionist, who manipulates his left shoulder. Bending it into one uncomfortable position after another.*]

PERFORMER: Hold it like that?

PERFECTIONIST: The initial injury was to the left side. When X-rayed –

PERFORMER: My shoulder blade?

PERFECTIONIST: ... the shoulder blade was shown to have been pushed down about half an inch. This caused a very troubling secondary reaction; the nerve which controls the fourth and fifth fingers of the left hand had been compressed and inflamed.

PERFORMER: The doctor in Toronto gave me cortisone shots

on alternating days … . no, it was worse than ever.

PERFECTIONIST: You became so obsessed with this pain in your shoulder that you went to see a very fancy neurologist at Johns Hopkins …

PERFORMER: A cast? Like this? Two months? Here? Alone? [*smile*] Yes. That sounds ideal.

PERFECTIONIST: At the end of it all Jessie phoned the neurologist to see how you were doing. The doctor said: 'Not a thing wrong with him. Physically'. Nevertheless, as a result of this little *divertimento* you were able to take leave of the concert stage for *six whole months*.

[*The Performer reacts with pleasure.*]

Not only that, you subsequently *sued* Steinway & Sons.

PERFORMER: I did?

PERFECTIONIST: Steinway & Sons paid.

[*He beams. The Performer hesitantly follows suit as he gets the picture. Lights fade. Another note from the ground bass.*]

Variation 15: This Is Where I Get Off

[*Sound: aircraft engines. Lights up on the Four Glenns sitting in a row of airline seats. The Prodigy and the Performer sit together on one side of the aisle, the Perfectionist and the Puritan sit across from them. The Performer and the Puritan have the aisle seats. The Prodigy and the Perfectionist are at the windows. All are rigid with fear.*]

FEMALE VOICE: [*American accent, off*] In preparation for landing please ensure that your seat belt is securely fastened and that your chair backs and tables are in the upright position. And thanks for flying American.

PERFECTIONIST: [*to Puritan*] The engine pitch changed.

PRODIGY: [*to Performer*] What was that bump?

PURITAN: [*to Perfectionist*] They put the wheels down.

PERFORMER: [*to Prodigy*] We're on our final approach.

> [*Sound: air pocket.*]

ALL: *Air pocket!*

PERFECTIONIST: [*whisper to Puritan*] I have a terrible secret. I'm the only one keeping us aloft. Without me the rest of you disintegrate in an enormous fire ball.

> [*The Perfectionist pops open an air sickness bag. The Puritan leans across the aisle to the Performer.*]

PURITAN: Would you mind if we changed seats? I just realized I'm in D. Very bad key for me.

PERFORMER: My pleasure.

> [*The Puritan and the Performer change seats. The Puritan is surprised and pleased to find himself sitting down beside the Prodigy. The Performer is less enthusiastic about his seat next to the Perfectionist.*]

PURITAN: [*to Prodigy*] First flight alone?

PERFORMER: [*to Perfectionist*] You're looking rather bilious.

> [*The Perfectionist puts away his air sickness bag.*]

PRODIGY: Yes it is.

PERFECTIONIST: Not you again –

PERFORMER: We're joined at the hip.

PURITAN: Afraid?

PERFECTIONIST: That's a terrifying thought.

PRODIGY: Terrified. You?

PERFORMER: I eat this fear for breakfast.

PURITAN: Speechless with anxiety.

PRODIGY: What if we die?

PERFECTIONIST: [*to Puritan*] Humour him. He's only a child.

PURITAN: We die a little bit every second we're alive.

> [*Sound: air pocket.*]

ALL: *Turbulence!*

> [*All four Glenns take their pulses.*]

PERFECTIONIST: [*to the entire row*] Talk of death is surely

premature. Might I suggest a simple exchange of pleas-
antries?

ALL: [*to their seat-mates*] Where you headed?

PERFECTIONIST: This is my final trip to New York.

PRODIGY: I'm giving up my piano lessons.

PERFORMER: I'm abandoning the concert stage.

PURITAN: I-I'm not sure where I'm headed.

PERFECTIONIST: Perhaps if we played the game we could
stabilize this situation – [*to the row*] Concentrate on images
of flight! If-if you were a-a bird what species would you
be?

PRODIGY: I'd be a budgie – safe and warm in mother's kitchen.

PERFORMER: A peregrine falcon – soaring high above the
Arctic wastes.

PERFECTIONIST: [*to Performer*] No! You're a bower bird –
trapped in your extravagant display.

PURITAN: [*indicating Performer*] I'd be a dodo – flightless, overly
specialized to the point of extinction.

PERFECTIONIST: My good man, 'extinction' is officially off-limits!

[*Sound: air pocket.*]

ALL: *Wind shear!*

PURITAN: [*to Prodigy*] Are those runway lights?

PRODIGY: What was that noise?

PERFORMER: [*to Perfectionist*] The flaps.

PERFECTIONIST: We'll be home before you know it.

ALL: This is it!

[*Everyone tenses and leans back as the plane comes in for a landing.*]

PRODIGY: Tell mother I loved her!

PERFORMER: A blinding flash of glory! *Perfect!*

PERFECTIONIST: My conscience is clear!

PURITAN: Not yet!

[*Snap to black. Music up: excerpt from Bach's Fourth Partita. Lights shift. The mood of the travellers has settled.*]

PRODIGY: Bach's Fourth Partita. Some day I'll play like that.

PERFECTIONIST: April 10, 1964, The Wiltshire Ebell Theatre in Los Angeles.

PERFORMER: My last public performance.

PERFECTIONIST: [*to Performer*] You bowed and I walked off the stage. Never to return.

PERFORMER: The end of all applause.

PURITAN: Surely one thing ends so another can begin.

[*Sound: tires hit runway. The Glenns bounce once as the plane lands, then applaud the pilot's skill. Audience applause continues, under.*]

ALL: First Rate! Outstanding! Superb! Bravo!

[*The applause continues as they come to their feet.*]

PRODIGY: [*to Perfectionist, finally getting it*] Are you … are you *Glenn Gould?*

PERFECTIONIST: Absolutely not.

PRODIGY: [*to the Performer*] Gould? Glenn Gould! The noted Canadian pianist.

PERFORMER: Never heard of him.

PRODIGY: [*to Puritan*] Glenn Gould!

PURITAN: Glenn Gould? Afraid not.

PRODIGY: You're all Gould, aren't you?

PURITAN, PERFORMER & PERFECTIONIST: This is where I get off.

> [*They exit. The Prodigy hesitates a beat, picks up the Puritan's copy of Kafka and runs off. Fade to black. Another note from the ground bass.*]

The Interval

Variation 16: The French Overture

[*Variation 16, early version, carries the audience into the interval. During the half-hour* Quiet in the Land, The Idea of North *and* The Latecomers *play in various lobby areas. The audience returns to the accompaniment of Variation 16, late version. At the end of the variation, lights fade. Another note from the ground bass.*]

Act Two

Variation 17: The Sound of Myself

[*Lights up: firelight flickers. The Prodigy enters reading a book.*]

PRODIGY: [*impressed by what he's just read*] Franzie-boy, you got it nailed! An artist must *remove* himself from the world! It's all right here! [*reading*] 'That is why one can never be alone enough when one writes, why there can never be enough silence when one writes. Why not even night is night enough.' Why not even *night* is night enough! Now, *this* guy knows how to have fun! I've got to get mother to read him! [*pause*] Sure thing …

[*He wanders to the keyboard. He plays a single note, listens to it fade.*]
The world sleeps while I read my Kafka.

[*Lights up on the Puritan who reclines on his lazy-boy chair, opposite.*]

PURITAN: No longer possible to play even a Bach chorale securely … parts unbalanced, progression from note to note insecure …

[*The Prodigy moves again, coming closer to the Puritan. They remain unaware of one another.*]

PRODIGY: Kafka smelled the rot in the world. [*looking at his hands*] If it weren't for this … I'd be a writer too. Roam the blank page with my perfect pitch and my sense of contrapuntal voicing. *The Longing*, a novella by Glenn Gould, Esquire. [*performing it*] 'He rose at dawn and' – no – 'he *stayed up* until dawn and watched light come into the land in tinctures of grey. He knew it was going to be a long day, so many stations of the cross before he … before he –' Nah. Too slow …

PURITAN: ... an unpleasant experience, seemingly immune to ad hoc pressures ...

PRODIGY: I can see the reviews: [*British accent*] *The Longing* is a precocious first novel about a great pianist near the end of his days – a brave old man seeking refuge from life's last riddle. Is Glenn Gould projecting a future for himself here? Only time will tell ...

[*He paces, thinking.*]

PURITAN: ... wrist tightness problems ... separation into bumpy groupings and a general lack of fluidity ...

PRODIGY: Never mind that. Sunday painters read their reviews – onward! Let me see: [*performing a line*] 'The great man prowls the endless night of the city, a solitary traveller on a path that leads relentlessly inward.'

PURITAN: ... right wrist unbearably sore after any ten to fifteen minute practice period ...

PRODIGY: And now his mother lies dying. He has come down from the mountain to be at her side.

PURITAN: ... the fingers should not be required to move ... only to *be there* ...

PRODIGY: The squeak of the stairs as he climbs toward her room. [*sotto voce*] So many things he must say to the dying woman.

PURITAN: Hear the blood in my brain ... the ringing ...

PRODIGY: She's sitting in a reclining chair under a plaid wool throw. She seems to be asleep, or perhaps not ...

PURITAN: ... nothing prevents a gradual deterioration of the mental image.

PRODIGY: 'Mother?'

[*The Puritan sits up. He has a cramp in his shoulder.*]

She turns to look at him. 'I am about to die,' she says, 'And that is as it should be. Why have you come to see me?'

[*The Puritan puts a thermometer in his mouth.*]

The old man exercises his legendary control. All the words must be in perfect order before he utters a syllable. He reaches into the glowing core of his being ...

[*The Puritan comes to his feet wearily, heads offstage*]

PURITAN: I must write to the makers of Fiorinal – '... when combined with a certain state of hyperactive exhaustion your product delivers a superb waking nightmare.'

[*Light shift. Another note from the ground bass.*]

Variation 18 : Actuality versus Realism

[*Sound: New York city street noise. The Perfectionist strolls into the light, pondering a yellow legal-length pad. He does not acknowledge the Puritan and the Prodigy.*]

PERFECTIONIST: '– superb waking nightmare.' Laughter. Right speaker fades.

[*The Puritan moves into shadow.*]

Left speaker –

PRODIGY: I'm doing what I said I always wanted to do. Why can't she understand?

PERFECTIONIST: [*circling a word on his pad*] Why *can't*? Why *won't*? Why *doesn't*? Wash from the Scherzo, and out.

[*Lights fade on the Prodigy. The Perfectionist paces, looks up and down the street at the noisy traffic.*]

The driver from Columbia was supposed to be here twenty minutes ago. This is absurd ... taxi!

[*Sound: louder street noise. He waves his arm as the taxi drives by. The Prodigy stays onstage.*]

Five years since I quit performing, you'd think I'd never have to travel against my will again. But nooo, that would be too easy. Every time I want to record I must make a nightmare pilgrimage to this ... this colossus that grinds human souls to powder. Taxi!

[*He waves his arm again. Watches another cab go by. Lights up on the Performer who sits in the lazy-boy chair under the plaid wool throw, jotting schematics on a yellow legal-length pad.*]

PERFORMER: The Central Conundrum: I give up public performance ... yet I still must perform for the public. [*writing*] The moment of infinite privacy surrendered naked to the scrutiny of strangers.

PERFECTIONIST: One seeks perfection and is rewarded with the experience of mob rule. [*looking around*] It sifts down on you all day long in Manhattan. The spiritual soot of America.

PERFORMER: [*writing*] The walls close in. The brain pressure is measured in tons-per-square-inch. [*thinking*] So, finally, the Performer must withdraw. He walks off the stage in Los Angeles and ends up in *this* chair at Uptergrove ... Question: What does the born performer *do* after he stops performing?

PERFECTIONIST: Where is Theodore Slutz when I need him most?

PERFORMER: [*in recognition*] Answer: He dons the disguise of the moment.

PERFECTIONIST: Taxi!

[*The Performer gets up from the chair.*]

PERFORMER: Dressed as a guard ... I walk backwards out of the prison. [*He puts on his 'Theodore Slutz hat'. Singing, New Jersey accent*] 'The buildin's reach up to the sky / Traffic thunders on the busy streets / Pavement slips beneath my feet / I sit alone and wonder / Who am I?'

PERFECTIONIST: [*spotting the Performer*] Finally, this fellow seems to have noticed me. Now all I have to do is cross six lanes of rush-hour traffic.

[*Sound: traffic noise up. The Perfectionist heads across the six lanes of traffic. It's a harrowing journey. He just makes it. Lights shift to favour the Prodigy as he enters the action.*]

PRODIGY: New York City! This time next month I'll be recording there. Got to get mentally prepared ...

[*He closes his eyes, does the 'taking flight' gesture, thinks better of it, then hustles over to retrieve his piano stool, realizing he'll need it in New York.*]

... imagine myself there in the best possible light. I swoop down on Central Park, the trees a nubbly lawn at my feet. Buildings bend around the bowl of the sky. I bank down Fifth Avenue ... come in for a landing at ... at Rockefeller Centre!

[*He 'lands' in Manhattan. Lights up on the Perfectionist and the Performer who are in mid-conversation. The Performer talks into his rear-view mirror.*]

PERFORMER: [*as Theodore Slutz, New Jersey accent*] – and poof! there's a cloud of magic pixie dust and this teensy-weensy grand piano appears with a concert pianist yea-big standing beside it. The guy at the bar turns to the genie and says: 'Hey, bubba! I didn't ask for a ten inch *pianist*.'

[*He cracks up. The Perfectionist smiles thinly. The Prodigy is gawking at the skyscrapers.*]

SLUTZ: A ten-inch pianist. It's a-a word thing –

PERFECTIONIST: Yes. I understand. Assonance.

SLUTZ: [*to rear-view mirror*] Why do you think I told you that joke?

PERFECTIONIST: Your reasoning, sir, is beyond me. The road, please.

SLUTZ: Because you're Glenn Gould! I read your occasionals in *High Fidelity Magazine*.

PERFECTIONIST: My-my, a subscriber – watch out!

[*Sound: squealing tires. The Performer swerves to miss the Prodigy, who is startled out of his reverie by the commotion. Sound: street noise, traffic and pedestrians, continuing under.*]

SLUTZ: A survivor, Mr Gould!

[*The Perfectionist is transfixed by the sight of the Prodigy.*]

Theodore Slutz, taxi driver, avant garde musician –

PERFECTIONIST: [*interrupting wearily*] – and music editor of *The Village Grass is Greener*. Your reputation precedes you, sir.

SLUTZ: That last piece you did about actuality and realism – very intense, Mr Gould, *very* personal, if you get what I mean.

PERFECTIONIST: [*interrupting*] The distinction between actuality and realism is fundamental to the creative act in the modern era. And my train to Toronto leaves in less than ten minutes.

[*He can't take his eyes off the Prodigy, who rubbernecks at the tall buildings.*]

SLUTZ: [*driving*] If I understand you correctly, actuality is like the-the rush of pure event.

PERFECTIONIST: Correct.

SLUTZ: And realism ...

PERFECTIONIST: Is an artificial event which can be infinitely manipulated by technology.

SLUTZ: Which is where your personal life comes in.

[*The Prodigy has caught up to them again. The Perfectionist is startled to see him.*]

PERFECTIONIST: I think not.

SLUTZ: [*accelerating*] You're a born performer, Mr Gould. The concert stage was your actuality and now you've withdrawn into this state of total realism.

PERFECTIONIST: Never thought of it quite that way.

SLUTZ: [*accelerating further*] You've disappeared into your own rule book, Mr Gould. [*over his shoulder*] What happens to the

Performer? Huh? Do you keep that part of yourself chained to a dungeon wall, or what?

[*He hammers the brakes. He and the Perfectionist rock forward as the cab squeals to a stop. The Prodigy makes a direct approach, aware of the cab for the first time. Opens the door.*]

PRODIGY: Excuse me, I-I'm looking for Columbia Masterworks, two-hundred and seven east Thirty Street.

SLUTZ: Get in, kid. [*to Perfectionist*] We can drop him on the way.

[*The Prodigy gets in.*]

PRODIGY: [*offering his hand to the Perfectionist*] I'm Glenn Gould.

[*The Perfectionist looks at the kid in horror.*]

SLUTZ: Check the gloves! Where you from kid, Greenland?

PRODIGY: Toronto, actually. That's in Canada. Everybody up there dresses like this in June.

PERFECTIONIST: That's very funny. [*to the driver*] What's going on here?

SLUTZ: All of this is happening in my head! I'm improvising on a riff!

PERFECTIONIST: I have a very limited appetite for improvisation. Like your little game here, it's mostly cliché. [*to the Prodigy*] What are you staring at?

PRODIGY: I'm afraid I-I've lost my way.

SLUTZ: [*rear-view mirror*] Remember?

PRODIGY: I thought I was imagining all this.

PERFECTIONIST: [*to Performer*] I have no idea what you're talking about.

SLUTZ: Neither end nor beginning. Neither climax nor resolution. The composition, like Baudelaire's lovers –

PERFECTIONIST: [*interrupting*] Utter gibberish! Stop this cab immediately!

SLUTZ: Skippin' town, right? Never coming back here to record.

PERFECTIONIST: That is the plan.

SLUTZ: You're gonna set up some kind of basement recording studio.

PERFECTIONIST: The Eaton Auditorium is hardly a basement.

SLUTZ: Sorry, GG. Bunker mentality.

[*The Prodigy has picked up on the negative energy between his cab mates.*]

PRODIGY: [*to the driver*] This is not what I expected.

PERFORMER: Larger than life! [*rear-view mirror*] Right, GG?

PERFECTIONIST: [*fed up*] Indeed. We apparently transcend the laws of physics. My train leaves in eight minutes. Grand Central Station is ten blocks from here. I'll do better on foot.

[*He clambers over the Prodigy's knees to get out of the taxi.*]

SLUTZ: [*after him*] Wash from the Scherzo and out, bubba!

PRODIGY: I'm a little ... lost.

SLUTZ: Relax, kid. Trust what you know. [*looking after the Perfectionist*] And don't trust it when you know too much. I'm afraid we haven't heard the last from that guy ...

PRODIGY: I-I was trying to get mentally prepared to record my first album –

SLUTZ: Beautiful, kid! That's beautiful. Prepare to fall in love!

[*He hands the Prodigy the album cover for his first recording of the Goldberg Variations. The kid is full of wonder. Lights shift. Another note from the ground bass.*]

Variation 19: Action at a Distance

[*Music under: Variation 19. The Puritan enters reading from a yellow legal-length pad.*]

PURITAN: To Herbert von Karajan. From Glenn Gould, Esquire. Subject: Proposal for a collaborative recording. Dear Maestro: As you know, for some time now I have been exploring the technological and philosophical implications of 'Action at a Distance' –

[*He writes on his pad. The Prodigy dances with a microphone. The Performer schlumfs in, still wearing his Theodore Slutz hat, sits down in front of a television set, peels back the foil on a TV dinner, clicks on the set and starts to eat.*]

PERFECTIONIST: [*on monitor*] Oh, I know what you're thinking. Here's old GG back to bend my ear with more tendentious twaddle about technology.

PURITAN: [*reading from his pad*] I believe it is easier for people to show their better natures to one another if they are not in close physical proximity. Technology makes this ideal possible.

[*He goes back to his writing.*]

PRODIGY: I'm having a love affair. With the microphone!

[*He waltzes with a microphone stand.*]

PERFECTIONIST: [*on monitor*] I've taken certain home truths about technology deeply to heart – it might not be a bad idea to have a pad and pencil handy in case you want to take a few notes –

[*The Performer goes to fetch writing implements. The Perfectionist bides his time.*]

PURITAN: Since I no longer travel by air it's been many years since we've met face to face. I regret this greatly.

PERFECTIONIST: [*on monitor*] Proposition: Technology now mediates between man and the aesthetic experience.

PURITAN: I must admit a certain longing for another opportunity to record with you as I did in my youth. Thus this modest proposal for a rather unique collaboration between us on the Beethoven Second. The creative parameters are as follows:

[*He makes notes. The Performer re-enters with a yellow pad and a pen, sits back down in front of the monitor, all ears. The Perfectionist smiles.*]

PERFECTIONIST: [*on monitor*] Corollary: Properly applied, home playback technology can liberate the performer and equip him for a dynamic new relationship with both his audience and his music!

PRODIGY: This is music that will stream across the sky!

[*He picks up his recording of the Goldberg Variations and begins to 'fly' it around the space.*]

PURITAN: Step One: GG and HvK discuss, via telephone, all the relevant interpretive aspects of the score – tempo, dynamic relationships and so on.

PERFECTIONIST: [*on monitor*] Free of the obligation to grind out he same pound of hamburger night after night on the concert stage, the 'New Performer' roams at will through musical literature, interprets it in the recording studio, then moves on to fresh challenges. At all points his view is panoramic!

PRODIGY: Lightly, on the wings of the unchecked wind!

[*Music under: Excerpt from Moonlight Sonata.*]

PURITAN: Step Two: GG proceeds to prerecord piano parts, editing a two-track sub-master, which would be appropriately leadered, either for tracking or a mix, for stop cues during tuttis.

[*The Prodigy flies his album around the space.*]

PERFECTIONIST: [*on monitor*] It's an error to see these constructs as Orwellian, a technocratic conspiracy designed to strip man of his humanity. In my view technology exercises a kind of invisible charity.

PRODIGY: A single farmhouse with one light on. The rink out front where kids were skating. My music pours from the kitchen radio.

PURITAN: Step Three: HvK would record the orchestral sections, using piano pretape.

PERFECTIONIST: [*on monitor*] The hierarchies of electromagnetic radiation are the unheard harmonics of consciousness itself. Technology is on the side of moral goodness and the sublime.

PRODIGY: The woman stops cooking, looks out the window into the darkening field ... cocks her head ... listening ...

PURITAN: Thesis and resolution: That HvK and GG can have a meeting of the minds ... without the meeting.

PRODIGY: We intertwine like Baudelaire's lovers ... my music defying time and space! A love letter to the world!
    [*Music out.*]

PERFECTIONIST: [*on monitor*] I see this interactive electronic complex as my playground ... and I look forward to having you on the other end of the teeter-totter.
    [*His broadcast ends. The Performer, aka Theodore Slutz, checks out his notes. Crumples them up in a ball.*]

PERFORMER: Nah.
    [*He tosses his notes at the monitor. The Perfectionist ducks.*]

PERFECTIONIST: You've forgotten how it was! I've seen the movie of your life, my friend. Remember Tel Aviv?
    [*The Puritan folds up his letter.*]

PURITAN: Anthithesis and retribution: The end result could sound God-awful. The Maestro won't go for this, not in a million years. He'll think I got off between floors. [*German accent*] Mr Gould, you are playing a game of mirrors. You can't be in two places at once! [*normal voice, making a discovery*] If one seeks unity with the ideal one must transcend mere technology. Something ... ineffable ... whispers from the deep place between the notes. [*whisper, in wonder*] Art ... on its loftiest mission ... is hardly ... human ... at all.

[*He looks at his hands. Light shift. Another note from the ground bass.*]

Variation 20: Tel Aviv: the Ideal Performance

[*The Perfectionist enters and moves to his studio chair.*]

PERFECTIONIST: I am always amused by the assumption that it is somehow fraudulent to splice together a perform-ance. That an artist's performance must always be the result of some unbroken forward *thrust*. Some sustained *animus*. Some *ecstatic high*. By my lights an ideal perform-ance reveals deep musical structure as a pure emotional line. If this 'ideal performance' can be better achieved with illusion and fakery, I say more power to those who can work that magic. The Tel Aviv Piano: Take Two! [*holding up two pieces of mag tape*] Sand Dune. Beethoven. [*whisper*] We hold the beating heart of the music in our bare hands –

[*He picks up a script, swivels in his chair and gestures to alter the light-ing for dramatic effect. The Performer enters, in a kind of daze. The Prodigy moves to the piano. The Perfectionist 'conducts' their entries and exits throughout, following his script, mouthing key words. Music under: Beethoven's Sonata No 30, Opus 109.*]

PRODIGY: I never listen to anything when I'm preparing to play Beethoven. Before Bach I listen to Strauss, Franck, Sibelius, juke boxes, anything. But nothing before Beeth-oven. I must go in like a horse with blinders.

PERFORMER: That stupid pig of a piano ...

PRODIGY: I always commit a new score to memory before I

go to the keyboard to keep expressive manifestations divorced from the tactilia. I don't want my fingers telling my brain what to do.

PERFORMER: I can't even remember what a real instrument *feels* like.

> [*He starts doing hand exercises to limber up the musculature of his fingers.*]

PRODIGY: There is a moment in Opus 109 which is a positive horror – an upward-bound diatonic run in sixths.

PERFORMER: Not even a C scale properly. I've got to *remember* ...

PRODIGY: It's an awkward moment not only in terms of black versus white note fingerings but also in terms of that break in the keyboard around two octaves above middle C – precisely the point where Mr Beethoven asks us to change from a pattern in sixths to a pattern in thirds. [*demonstrating the riff*] Sixths ... to this ... and you've got to do it in a split second.

PERFORMER: ... find the moment somewhere ... get inside it.

> [*He tenses in on himself.*]

PRODIGY: I had always heard this piece played by people who, when the moment of truth arrived, acted like horses in a burning barn –

PERFECTIONIST: [*cueing the Performer*] The deep emotional line!

> [*The Performer does the 'taking flight' gesture.*]

PERFORMER: Uptergrove! The Chickering!

PRODIGY: A week before the concert I decided it was time to sit down and play the piece through for the first time.

> [*The Perfectionist conducts with building energy, vocalizing words and phrases when he can't control himself.*]

Suicidal, [*with Perfectionist*] but that's the way I always do things. [*solo*] The first thing I did, foolishly – very bad psychology – was to say: 'Well, let's try that tricky bit of fingering, [*with Perfectionist*] work out a little keyboard routine, just in case.'

PERFORMER: Light streams through the trees beyond the window ... hold and refine the mental image ... enter the time and space it occupies. *Be there.*

PRODIGY: And as I began to work out my system one thing after another went wrong. Before many minutes had elapsed I'd developed a total mental block. [*with building anxiety*] I just froze at that particular moment.

PERFECTIONIST: [*cueing the Performer*] The lame can walk!

PERFORMER: I move toward the keyboard ...

PRODIGY: I'm in the burning barn!

[*The Performer recoils in shock; this is not what he came for.*]

PERFECTIONIST: Stand by –

PRODIGY: Then I tried the last resort method!

PERFORMER: [*trying to convince the Prodigy*] ... the unheard music!

PERFECTIONIST: [*preparing to cue, under*] Aaaaand –

PRODIGY: [*overlapping Perfectionist*] I put a couple of radios on the piano and turned them up full blast!

PERFECTIONIST: [*cueing*] GO! The charity of the machine! Ecstasy!

[*The Prodigy and the Performer are transported. A unifying physical gesture. Ecstasy! Sound: complex radio overlay. Chunks of strange language hurtle by – BBC World Service. Radio Valpariso. A soccer game from Karachi. Snippets of martial music from the Soviet Bloc. Light shift. Another note from the ground bass.*]

Variation 21: The Canadian Unconscious

[*Sound: radio overlay shifts and continues, under. Lights fade on the Prodigy and the Performer.*]

PERFECTIONIST: I'm doing a radio documentary that examines the effects of solitude and isolation upon those who live in the Arctic ...

PURITAN: Radio has always been of fundamental importance to Canadians and in that sense my current residency at the CBC is a kind of homecoming.

PERFECTIONIST: ... the people never actually meet ... the texture of the words themselves differentiate the characters and create dream-like conjunctions within the documentary.

PURITAN: Ours is a vast country, tenuously bound together by technology. In some subtle way the northern latitudes seem to have a modifying influence on our national character.

PERFORMER: A Russian doll approach to composition. Narrative nesting inside narrative in a documentary that thinks of itself as a drama.

PURITAN: To make a sweeping generalization, I think Canadians have a synoptic view of the world we live in. And in that regard I consider the Idea of North a kind of national anthem, you know, chamber music for the Canadian unconscious ...

[*The radio collage stops. Sound: thwacketa-thwacketa-thwacketa of broken mag tape.*]

PERFECTIONIST: [*cueing his engineer*] Stop tape!

[*The Perfectionist looks at the Prodigy and the Performer. Both are in disarray. He turns to smile at the camera.*]

No cause for alarm. We leave nothing to chance here in Studio G, even the disasters are scripted. Unity. Cohesion.

Structure. These are the things that matter most to us. I think we've made our point. It's all perfectible. There are no limits. Total control is the balance point. [*turning off the camera*] These beliefs we bind to us with hoops of steel ...

[*Light shift. Another note from ground bass.*]

Variation 22: Behaviour and Belief: a fugue state

[*Lights up: the Puritan is in his chair. He comes suddenly awake and sits upright, moving his right hand up and down his left arm from wrist to shoulder, administering little squeezes to relieve pain.*]

PURITAN: In the dream ... I awaken in a dream. It is the night before some ancient battle. Campfires dot the hillside. Soldiers, awaiting my instruction ...

[*One by one minimal light comes to the other playing areas. The Perfectionist enters on the phone, listening, nodding, then saying 'uh-huh, uh-huh'. He moves to his studio chair, repeating the sequence again and again. The Prodigy sits at the keyboard and 'plays' a modulated quote from Variation 22 – a single musical phrase twisted into a seductive mœbius. The musical figure has caught the Prodigy in its thrall. He repeats it again and again, a stuck needle. As he repeats the musical phrase he repeats the series of physical moves involved in its playing and vocalizes under the notes. The Performer, meanwhile, stands in the Prodigy's playing area with a reel of 35 mm film. He unspools it a yard at a time, a rhythmic gesture, as he 'reads frames'. His breathing is audible, his attention intense. A sense of pleasure and pain. The Puritan focuses on the building wash of sound around him in the semi-darkness. He gets up from his chair. Uneasy.*]

PURITAN: Before taking the field a warrior must anneal his sword in the fires of his deepest beliefs.

[*He pauses, listening.*]

PERFORMER: Concert hall audiences want that moment of ecstatic release – they want to feel the pain of 'the other' – the most primitive human secrets worn on the performer's face. The French call it 'the little death'. I'll show you what I mean ...

[*He unspools more film stock, looking for footage. The Prodigy's performance continues to build in intensity.*]

PERFECTIONIST: [*jovial*] ... darling, it gets worse! [*reading letter*] 'When I heard you that night so long ago in Fort Worth' – remember now, this woman is talking about something

that happened *nine years ago* – 'I felt a rush of primitive carnal energy –' [*laughing*] I'm sorry, darling, I can't – *a rush of primitive carnal energy?* They're putting something in this woman's drinking water! I'm getting three of these letters a week! What am I to *do*?

[*He listens. The Prodigy's performance continues to build. The Puritan writes on his pad.*]

PERFORMER: This is what I see: [*he 'reads' a sequence of frames*] The African veldt. Sere grasslands to the horizon. Acacia trees shift and shunt in the mirage while a pride of lions tugs loose the viscera of a standing wildebeest. Thirty feet of shining intestine.

> [*He is transfixed by the horror of his own description. For a moment the film stock becomes the intestine.*]

PERFECTIONIST: You don't understand, darling. I've never met this woman and she wants me to go and live on her cattle ranch in Texas.

> [*The Prodigy's playing of the phrase contorts with anxious complexity.*]

PERFORMER: The wildebeest stands splay-legged, motionless in the heat. There is nothing now but this. The shock and ecstasy of public disembowelment.

PERFECTIONIST: Of course she's entitled to her feelings. But is that a license to *consume* me?

PERFORMER: He watches, wild-eyed, while the big cats settle to feed in the wash of his blood. This is what the audience came for. Blood and sand. Catharsis ancient as the brain stem.

PURITAN: STOP!

> [*Music out. Perfectionist, Prodigy and Performer go into a freeze. The Puritan moves toward the piano.*]

I believe a musical performance is not a contest but a love affair and that love affairs must be conducted in private. I believe that public performance is the last blood sport and that applause is a shallow externalized expression of brute herd instinct: the howling mob is composed of passive individuals and passivity is the enemy of art. [*with growing conviction*] I believe that everything that is involved with virtuosity and exhibitionism on the platform is outward looking, or causes, outward lookingness, and that that is sinful, to use an old-fashioned word. I believe that the purpose of art is the active life-long construction of a state of wonder and serenity.

[*He gestures toward the Prodigy, who begins to play again. Calmer now. The Puritan addresses himself to the Performer.*]

Morality has never been on the side of the carnivore. Consciousness abhors bloodshed.

[*The Performer begins to guiltily gather up his film stock. The Puritan pauses, watches the Prodigy, thinking.*]

The deep question is: *Why* do I believe as I do? Because my beliefs are true ... or because I need them for reasons that are forever lost in the rear-view mirror? The emotional line runs deeper still ... the warrior must see himself in a new light ... he must learn to *listen* ...

[*He gestures, cueing the Prodigy. The Prodigy begins to play again. The Puritan listens, then gestures again to silence the Prodigy.*]

He doesn't know where he is.

[*He gestures toward the Performer. The Performer gathers up his film stock. The Puritan indicates the Performer.*]

He doesn't know where he's going.

[*He gestures again. The Perfectionist comes out of his freeze.*]

PERFECTIONIST: What do you mean, darling? I brought this up because I think you're the closest person in the whole [*pause*] ... darling, please ... please don't cry ... I'm so sorry ... I should have ... I know, darling, I know. [*suddenly nervous*] Jessie just arrived, darling. I'm going to have to – I'll call you tomorrow. [*hangs up and turns, he tries to smile*] Well, Jessie, where have we been?

[*The smile falters.*]

Yes, I am rather distressed. I was just talking to my dear, dear friend in Los Angeles. She brought it to my attention that it's two years since we broke off our relationship and I'm still calling her every day to compare intimacies. She accuses me of emotional manipulation. I must admit to a certain amount of confusion about her charges at the present moment.

PURITAN: [*indicating the Perfectionist*] He doesn't know where he's been.

PERFECTIONIST: If I really love her I'm supposed to let her go and pretend there's nothing between us … I'm sorry … I can't … I can't *hear* that just now …

[*He turns away from Jessie while he regains himself.*]

PURITAN: Silence. Time is suspended. One listens to … the inner self of the sound – in the deep place between the notes –

[*The Perfectionist turns back to Jessie. He's still distraught.*]

the sound of the inner self.

PERFECTIONIST: Sometimes I catch a fleeting glimpse of myself, Jessie. My eyes in the rear-view mirror as I drive the streets of this city at three am, music at grand volume on the tape deck. I'm not going anywhere in particular, I'm just moving from here to there and back again … a solitary figure in a landscape of sound …

[*Lights fade on Puritan. Another note from the ground bass. The Puritan exits.*]

Variation 23: Conducting the Self / Self-conduct

PRODIGY: [*entering on phone*] Jessie, sorry to call so early. Solitude makes one strangely convivial. It's like eating a pomegranate alone, one longs to turn to one's neighbour and compare notes. [*pause*] I know it's five in the morning, I've inverted my sleep cycle! I go to bed at dawn, wake up when the light is beautiful between the trees. [*responding to her worry*] I know, Jessie …

PURITAN: [*entering on phone*] I know, Susan, it's radical! I can be in two places at once! It's a whole new way of seeing myself!

PRODIGY: Jessie, I called because I feel like I've finally found a way to *see* myself –

PURITAN: That's right, conducting *and* playing at the same time, Susan, on Beethoven's Piano Concerto Number One. First, I conduct to the piano entry –

[*He sings the orchestral part.*]

PRODIGY: I was playing the Rondo from Beethoven's Concerto Number One on the Chickering – fishtailing through it at breakneck speed.

PURITAN: And then –

PRODIGY: [*overlapping Puritan*] Instead of –

[*They both sing the opening bars of the piano entry at a stately tempo.*]

It was –

[*He speeds up, singing the Rondo at breakneck speed.*]

It started to come in such a rush that I stepped outside the playing! Uh-huh –

PURITAN: [*finishing*] Right! And then I go back to my conducting – two-two-two Goulds in one! Uh-huh.

PRODIGY: I was hearing all the harmonics! I can't explain it, Jessie. The focus pulled way, way back. I was looking at myself across a great distance. I'm a person who makes sounds, Jessie. And by making sounds I show people how I hear. Isn't that a strange thing to do with your life?

[*Sound: phone rings.*]

PURITAN: [*cupping receiver, calling off*] Jessie? That's my private line in the kitchen, could you take a message? Except if it's that fellow from Juilliard [*into phone*] – sorry, Susan, I've been rambling on here. My question to you is, if I make this thing fly do you think Columbia will be interested?

PRODIGY: No, I'll wait. Go to the kitchen and make tea. I'll go back to planning my novel. [*reading his notes*] Chapter

Twenty-three. 'As he nears his fiftieth year the ageing virtuoso decides it's time to pass the torch to the next generation. He arranges for a prodigy to come and record with him, promising the lad he'll teach him everything he knows about playing the piano ...'

PURITAN: [*laughing*] Von Karajan once told me: [*German accent*] You assume control by being in control. [*normal*] Oh, that it were so simple! [*laughs again*] I think I may have reached an age where I know too much, Susan – a perilous state!

PRODIGY: 'The lad's name is Stephen Prince' – no, too direct – 'Stephen *Price*, the most promising student at Juilliard. With his heart in his mouth the boy telephones the great man to make the necessary arrangements –'

PURITAN: Susan, I love talking to you but I've got to go. My cousin Jessie has made tea. Right, mm-hm. [*he hangs up. To Jessie*] Juilliard? Drat. They have a volunteer for that little recording session I told you about. I've been waiting for his call. Hm? [*a darkening mood*] Jessie, I'm sorry, we've been over this. I've given it due consideration and I am not, repeat *not*, interested in *any* form of birthday celebration. [*pause*] It's not a question of health! I feel fine! I simply refuse to be trapped by that kind of chronology. The calendar is a tyrant! Once you submit to its relentless linearity you're ... you're *finished*. No cake. No candles. Understand? Go. Call my father. Tell him.

> [*Sound: telephone rings. The Prodigy reacts. His imagination has connected, lightly on the wings of the unchecked wind. The Puritan moves to answer the telephone.*]

Ah, Stephen Price. I've been waiting for your call. I'm thrilled that you've agreed to go along with my little experiment. Now, as to dates –

PRODIGY: [*still turned away from Puritan*] 'When the old man answers the boy is awestruck. He can hear himself babbling.'

PURITAN: Nonsense, Stephen, you're helping *me* fulfill a life-long dream to conduct. I'll make this promise to you – come to Toronto and I'll teach you everything you need to know about playing the piano in half an hour. The twenty-seventh Stephen. I'll have my people send you a ticket.

[*He hangs up the phone, thinks, smiles, writes on his pad. The Prodigy writes on his pad. The lights fade on them.*]

PRODIGY: [*into phone*] Jessie, you're back – what I'm trying to say is that I really think there's a way I can live! I'm starting to see myself in the future, and I like what I see ... I'm growing up, Jessie. I'm finally learning how to conduct myself!

[*Another note from the ground bass. Lights fade. The Prodigy moves centre stage, poised in his command of an imaginary audience.*]

Variation 24: The Centipede

[*The Prodigy moves toward the keyboard, brimming with confidence, fully in command of the moment. He sits on the special stool, slumps momentarily as he enters the psychological envelope.*]

PURITAN: [*from shadow*] You were born to perform.

PERFORMER: [*from shadow*] Fish swim, birds fly. You play the piano.

PERFECTIONIST: [*from shadow*] It's a glorified typewriter. Don't even think about the keys.

[*The Prodigy makes an extravagant gesture to indicate that sublime concentration of energy before the first note is struck. Snap to black. Music up: Prokofiev. The music is interrupted by sound cluster 1: a raging fire. Sirens whoop and wail. A police radio crackles: 'We got a three alarm at the Eaton auditorium on College.' Lights up: the Perfectionist crosses in front of the Prodigy, face in hands. The Prodigy reacts with dismay.*]

PERFORMER: The best way to solve a problem is not to think about it!

PURITAN: Focus on the whole, not the parts!

[*Snap to black. More Prokofiev. Music out. Sound cluster 2: workmen shout harried instructions as they lose control of a crated grand piano 'Take it easy, this is Gould's piano. Watch it!* WATCH IT!' *The piano lands with a crash of splintering wood, a broken chord. Lights up: the Performer kneels in front of the Prodigy, face in hands. The Prodigy reacts with horror, goes into a freeze, fingers touching temples. Light shift to the Puritan in his Eames chair.*]

Schoenberg once said that he would not be willingly asked by any of his composition students exactly why such and such a process served him well because that question made him feel like the centipede who was asked in which order it moved its hundred legs ... and afterwards could move no legs at all.

[*Sound: Sound cluster 3: the beep-beep-beep of a life support system. The voice of a doctor: 'The family has asked us to disconnect all life support. We're to let her go.' The Puritan reacts with grief, comes to his feet and moves into shadow, face in hands. Lights fade on the Prodigy. He looks at his hands. Another note from the ground bass.*]

Variation 25: Loss

[*Lights up on a series of images. Music up: 25th Variation, late version. Playing area 1: the Eames chair. The Puritan presides, writing on his yellow legal-length pad. Playing area 2: a hospital bed. The Perfectionist in residence, propped up facing the audience. Playing area 3: the keyboard, the Prodigy stands, lost in feeling.*]

PRODIGY: I was playing the piano beside the picture window this afternoon. A cardinal flew against the glass right in front of my face ...

[*Sound: fish sting.*]

PERFECTIONIST: She never *really* understood in those days, Jessie. She wanted things just so and ... [*small laugh*] I suppose I was a cocky little so and so ...

PRODIGY: ... its body landed in the snow. I sat there and waited for the bird to recover.

[*He sits on the piano stool.*]

PERFECTIONIST: We cared too much. That was our problem.

PURITAN: [*writing*] In late summer conducted experiments with elevated wrists. These inaugurated to alleviate unnatural burden in indented fingers, thumbs and knuckles.

[*The Prodigy waits for the cardinal to recover.*]

PERFECTIONIST: I remember once I came home from school expecting to find her in the kitchen putting my lunch on the table – tomato soup, peanut butter and honey, and glass of skim – yunno, *the* lunch. I came in the door and ... she wasn't there.

[*The Performer enters, sees the Perfectionist in his sick bed, pauses to watch him.*]

I went all through the house looking for her, calling for her. No answer. Well, this panic overcame me. I was a little boy and mummy wasn't where she was supposed to be. I was crying by the time I found her in the back garden. I went up to her, just mad as the dickens, and said: Mummy, *promise* me that you will never die! [*pause*] She promised.

PRODIGY: Two full minutes. No movement. Just the wind in its breast feathers.

PURITAN: The experiment resulted in a complete loss of control.

PRODIGY: [*coming to his feet*] I went out into the snow in my stocking feet. Four o'clock, a February afternoon in Ontario. That beautiful light between the trees.

[*The Prodigy bends in a slow gesture of grief.*]

PURITAN: [*'narrating' the Prodigy's move*] Tried holding wrist tightly from beneath so as to use it as fulcrum-like constant. At the same time tipping the head towards right shoulder and moving it as a unit so the fingers would be there when needed.

PRODIGY: I picked up the broken bird, such a wild exclamation of colour –

PURITAN: One day wonder.

PRODIGY: – carried him back inside. I've been playing the 25th Variation over and over again ever since ... fitting it to the mood of the moment ... the wistful and weary core of this day ...

PURITAN: No longer possible to play even Bach chorale securely.

PRODIGY: ... slowing it down ... relaxing the moments between the notes.

PURITAN: Parts were unbalanced, progression from note to note insecure.

PRODIGY: ... opening a space for his final flight.

PURITAN: Nothing prevents the gradual deterioration of image.

PRODIGY: There's no such thing as 'going too slow' in a moment like that.

PERFECTIONIST: She was in the dream I had last night, Jessie. She was sitting in the window chair at Uptergrove watching a bird at the feeder. She turned when she heard me enter the room. 'I am about to die and that is as it should be,' she said, 'Why have you come to see me?'

  [*He extends his hand to the Performer. The Performer moves to comfort the Perfectionist. It is an act of compassion and surrender.*]

[*reminding himself*] I believe in the hereafter, Jessie. I believe that all the spiritual energy that has ever been is with us now, radiant and invisible. We must not confuse ourselves with these bodies. I am not this body. I am an electromagnetic field that *animates* this body. Our atoms were forged inside exploding stars. Think of it, Jessie. [*looking at his hands*] Billions upon billions of years old.

[*Lights fade on them.*]

PRODIGY: The cardinal is on the kitchen table in a Birks box. When dawn comes I'm going to bury him like an Egyptian pharaoh. In the meantime, there is a grace note in this silence. The tone of the experience without the experience itself. I stand in the nave of Bach's cathedral. I listen.

[*Sound: the moan of Arctic wind. We hold this image for a couple of beats. Lights fade. Another note from the ground bass.*]

Variation 26: The Psychological Sub-text

[*The Perfectionist remains alone in his hospital bed under the covers. The Puritan makes a vaudeville entrance da-daing his way through 'Be Kind to Your Web-footed Friends / for a duck may be somebody's mother'. He rolls the Perfectionist's bed around.*]

PURITAN: Good evening, and welcome to another edition of 'Brain Peelers'! My name is Glenn Gould and my guest this evening is Dr Wolfgang von Krankmeister, the editor of *Insight*, the Journal of the North Dakota Psychiatric Association. Our subject this evening, that kooky Canadian virtuoso, Glenn Gould!

[*He tries to pull off the Perfectionist's sheet.*]

PERFECTIONIST: [*as Krankmeister, German accent*] Vat a pity. I come prepared to talk about Franz Kafka.

[*The Arctic wind stops, replaced by violin schmaltz from a Prague café, circa 1920.*]

PURITAN: Kafka is next week, Dr von Krankmeister. This is the twenty-sixth.

[*The Arctic wind and the Prague violin music commingle and continue throughout, under.*]

What we're trying to understand here are Glenn Gould's career choices.

KRANKMEISTER: Da psychological sub-text –

PURITAN: Precisely ... could we roll footage?

[*He cues the Performer. The Performer plays out his dialogue with an ironic edge; he's delivering the Perfectionist's words back to him.*]

PERFORMER: [*on monitor*] Proposition. Solitude is the prerequisite for ecstatic experience and the condition of heroism. Monastic seclusion works for me.

[*He holds his binoculars to his ear and scans the horizon.*]

KRANKMEISTER: Da typical schizoid dilemma! Desperate need for luf combines vis da equally desperate fear of da close involvement. Vhen Kafka enters his private prison in Prague he –

[*He dives back under the covers. The Puritan tries to secure an arm or a leg.*]

PURITAN: Forget Kafka! I want to get at the root of Gould's bravery.

[*He cues the Performer on a television monitor, pulls the Perfectionist out of bed by the legs. The Perfectionist struggles heroically.*]

PERFORMER: One can't feel oneself heroic without having first been cast off by the world, or better still, by having done the casting off oneself.

[*The Perfectionist is on his back on the floor now.*]

KRANKMEISTER: Vat's your point?

PURITAN: Proust said: 'Everything great comes from neurotics. They alone have founded religions and produced our masterpieces.'

[*He tries to pull the Perfectionist to his feet.*]

KRANKMEISTER: Patent nonsense. [*slithering under the bed*] Gould retreats from da verlt zo to obey laws of his own personality vich in da 'normal context' threaten to tear him apart!

[*The Puritan tows the Perfectionist across the floor, crashes offstage. Re-enters and makes another move on his adversary.*]

PURITAN: I would maintain that Gould neutralized his neurosis by turning it into vaudeville. His gift was an act of extreme extroversion – he had an overpowering need to dramatize his dilemma. Witness his invention of you, Herr von Krankmeister.

KRANKMEISTER: Behavioural disorganization and neurosis follows vhen introversion or extroversion gets out of whack –

PURITAN: But what if Gould's need to distance himself from others was an aspect of his quest to make a coherent pattern of his inner life?

KRANKMEISTER: You zound like one of my patients! Introvert-extrovert! Extrovert-introvert! Flip-flopping around like a fish on da dock! And da hypochondria – !

PURITAN: You think Gould was a hypochondriac?

[*He begins to dress the Perfectionist in overcoat, hat, muffler, gloves.*]

KRANKMEISTER: Hypochondria is an expression of his doubts about da validity of his own existence and fears dot others vill overwhelm and destroy him! Alienation from da body is characteristic of da schizoid personality.

PURITAN: Surely environmental factors have something to do with it. The man is quintessentially Canadian.

[*He cues the Performer.*]

PERFORMER: That genius flourishes in isolation is a notion foreign to the Canadian psyche. We distrust our own solitude. We're not a nation of doers, we're a nation of evaluators.

KRANKMEISTER: Zee? Gould *hated* evaluation! He vas estranged from his country!

PURITAN: Like I say, *quintessentially* Canadian. But you're missing the point. Gould honestly believed it was possible for people to show their better natures to one another without –

KRANKMEISTER: [*interrupting*] Keep da verlt at arm's length! Dis is Mr Control Freak again!

PURITAN: [*cueing the Performer*] You're not *listening*!

PERFORMER: Our benign neglect has left the north in something of a state of grace. Canada has never come to grips with the mental frontiers of its own geography. I, for one, feel whole in this empty landscape. I believe that all men who encounter it in solitude become, for want of a better word, philosophers.

[*Lights fade on the Performer.*]

PURITAN: You see, in Mr Gould's writings –

KRANKMEISTER: [*interrupting*] The octopus squirts ink to hide himself! Dis is nothing but damage control!

PURITAN: I guess you know a thing or two about that –

PERFECTIONIST: [*out of character*] What's that supposed to mean?

PURITAN: What happened there? Your accent –

PERFECTIONIST: I'm afraid this little game of yours has become rather tiresome. If you'll excuse me –

[*He starts his exit.*]

PURITAN: [*after him*] The truth about your friend Mr Gould is that he lives in great psychological pain.

PERFECTIONIST: [*exiting*] The truth about *your* Mr Gould is that he is about to die.

[*The lights begin to fade. The schtick is over now. The Puritan is utterly alone in this moment. He looks at his hands. Lights fade further. Another note from the ground bass.*]

Variation 27: The Homecoming

[*The Puritan studies his hands, lost in thoughts of mortality. The Prodigy enters, unseen and unannounced. He wears the trademark cap, overcoat, scarf and gloves. He stands where he is, watching the master in absolute awe. The Prodigy can't help himself; he kneels, cap in hand.*]

PRODIGY: [*as Stephen Price, New Jersey accent*] Mr Gould?

[*The Puritan turns, startled.*]

PURITAN: Who are you?

PRICE: Stephen Price.

[*The Puritan just stares.*]

The front door was open. I-I had a bet on with some kids at the dorm. I said: 'I'll get down on my hands and knees in front of the guy and do two 'Allahs'.'

PURITAN: 'Allahs'?

PRICE: Sorry, about this – it's worth twenty bucks. [*prostrating himself*] Allah. Allah.

[*The Puritan watches all of this, bemused.*]

PURITAN: Why are you dressed like that?

PRICE: You got a bit of a following at Juilliard.

PURITAN: I'm a style sample, am I?

PRICE: We think you got a few moves.

PURITAN: [*laughing*] That's really very funny.

PRICE: I'm serious! It's not just the look. Everybody *listens* to you. There are these heated debates.

PURITAN: I'll bet there are.

[*He starts laughing again. He can't help himself.*]

PRICE: – and we play the game.

PURITAN: Which one?

PRICE: I'm thinking of someone, guess who it is.

PURITAN: [*really enjoying this*] Don't start! *Please!*

PRICE: I had so many questions. About music. About what you believe. My mind's gone blank.

PURITAN: Performance anxiety. The hemispheres of the brain fall out of synchronicity. Are you familiar with the work of Julian Jaynes?

PRICE: *The Origin of Consciousness in the Breakdown of the Bicameral Mind?* Interesting book, the corpus callosum and all that, but I don't think God was an audio hallucination.

PURITAN: [*sitting in the Perfectionist's chair*] An intriguing hypothesis, nonetheless. If consciousness itself is an expression of the Deity's intent, which I tend to believe it is, then the coded recognition of that fact would be embedded in our brain physiology and transmitted to us in a multiplicity of ways. Hearing would quite naturally be one of them.

PRICE: I see what you're saying, music is sacred stuff.

PURITAN: Music, fog horns, branches tapping against windows in old Trevor Howard movies, a vacuum cleaner next door – they're all part of the Deity's message.

PRICE: Except music is art. The message is *about* itself.

PURITAN: Is that how you know something's art? Because it's *about* itself?

PRICE: That-that's one way of knowing. What do you think art is?

PURITAN: A life force released *by* the noblest aspirations in man and addressed *to* the noblest aspirations in man, his conscious desire for contact with the sublime. For transcendence.

PRICE: And music?

PURITAN: Are you getting this down on tape or something?

PRICE: It-it's a real question. I promised them I'd ask you.

PURITAN: Music is a pulse of intense feeling that illuminates the means of its own transmission. A kind of pure speech for the inner ear. When I was a little boy I could sight read from score and hear music which I had no way of playing because my hands were too small.

PRICE: Right!

PURITAN: I played it anyway, and sang the music the way I wanted to hear it when I couldn't reach the notes.

PRICE: The *unheard* music!

PURITAN: [*intrigued*] You've heard it?

PRICE: It's what makes me believe in the world.

[*They smile, knowing instinctively that some test has been passed.*]

PURITAN: Well, you're here. I'm here. We might as well get on with it. I have a few things to tell you that you may not be ready to hear.

PRICE: [*out of accent*] You promised you'd teach me everything you knew about playing the piano in –

PURITAN: [*interrupting*] What happened there? Your accent –

PRICE: [*back in accent*] What?

PURITAN: Say 'piano'.

PRICE: Piana. [*pause*] How are you going to teach me? I'll do anything you say. Is it like an exercise?

[*The Puritan looks at his hands.*]

PURITAN: I have nothing to teach you about this. Playing the piano is a way of thinking. You'll see how I think when we record together.

PRICE: I'll do whatever you say.

PURITAN: You'd better hear me out before you agree so readily. You and I are going to record the Beethoven Second Concerto ...

[*Music under: ten seconds before the piano entry in the second movement.*]

PRICE: I know. It's going to be *outrageous*. You *own* that Concerto. You played it for your orchestral debut with Bernstein.

PURITAN: And you are going to try and play the adagio section, *very* adagio, even slower than I played it. So slowly that the structure almost falls apart. You're going to invite me into the deep place between the notes.

PRICE: I'll play it as slow as you want, Maestro.

PURITAN: Don't call me 'maestro'.

PRICE: What do I call you then?

PURITAN: You call me Glenn.

[*They look at each other for a moment. The Prodigy has to look away.*]

PRICE: Just tell me what to do.

PURITAN: Now, I know that you came here because you wanted to play with Glenn Gould.

PRICE: It's the dream of a lifetime.

PURITAN: I'm afraid I must tell you that after we've finished recording I'm going to remove your performance and replace it with my own.

PRICE: Oh.

PURITAN: Everybody has their dream. Yours is to play with Glenn Gould. Mine is to conduct myself at the piano. We want different aspects of the same thing ... I hope you're not too disappointed.

PRICE: [*out of accent*] No. I-I'm not confused about –

PURITAN: [*interrupting*] There it is again. I hear Canada in your voice.

PRICE: No, sir.

PURITAN: No, *Glenn*.

[*He looks into the Prodigy's eyes. The Prodigy looks away.*]

Have you decided on a course for your career?

PRICE: I've been asked to play in Europe three months from now.

PURITAN: Bravo!

PRICE: I-I don't know if I'm ready.

PURITAN: Follow the unheard music. If it takes you to Europe, so be it.

PRICE: I ... I wish I was brave like you.

[*The comment brings the Puritan up short.*]

PURITAN: Brave men stand in front of bullets. I'm afraid that's not my –

PRICE: [*interrupting*] You're the bravest man I know.

PURITAN: Fish swim. Birds fly. I … I have played the piano.

[*The Prodigy hits a silent note on the keyboard. They both hear it.*]

PRICE: Never stop. Okay?

PURITAN: We'll do our best to … to carry on.

PRICE: Can I ask you a personal question?

PURITAN: Depends what it is …

PRICE: Are you happy?

PURITAN: Sorry. Indirect questions only, please.

PRICE: If I was you, what would I be?

PURITAN: A man looking back at himself. [*pause*] Don't be afraid. Go to Moscow.

[*Pause.*]

PRICE: You *knew*.

PURITAN: Of course I knew.

PRICE: I knew you knew.

PURITAN: [*little smile*] And I knew you knew I knew.

[*He hands the Prodigy a rose, and moves away from him, using the rear-view mirror gesture.*]

Let me see your smile …

[*The two men look into each other's eyes. The Prodigy smiles.*]

PRICE: Godspeed …

PURITAN: And you too …

[*Lights fade. Another note from the ground bass.*]

Variations 28-29: Mr Deeth

[*Lights up. The Perfectionist enters, buttoning the Performer into a white satin tuxedo shirt fitted and fastened with a hundred black dome*] *tabs. The shirt is a cross between evening wear and a strait-jacket. The Performer seems at ease.*]

PERFORMER: Not nearly tight enough. It won't do the job unless it's snug as a bug.

PERFECTIONIST: [*very cheerful*] Oh, you'd be surprised – a strong, well-disciplined mind can prevent its own disruption under almost any circumstances [*tightening the bonds*] – how's that?

PERFORMER: Perfection!

PERFECTIONIST: There's great freedom within total control.

PERFORMER: You're telling me! I could fly like a bird! How about a duet?

PERFECTIONIST: The game? This isn't a canon.

PERFORMER: Who cares? C'mon, just for old time's sake …

PERFECTIONIST: Got somebody in mind? I'm all ears.

PERFORMER: No. You go.

[*While the Perfectionist thinks he dum-dums to the unheard music.*]
You always do that when you're trying to know.

PERFECTIONIST: I don't *try* to know, my friend, I *know*.

PERFORMER: If you were a funeral, what kind of funeral would you be?

[*The question knocks the Perfectionist off-balance. He turns away from the Performer. Lights up on the Puritan, sitting in the lazy-boy chair under a plaid wool throw. He drowsily awakens from a dream.*]

PURITAN: I was receiving an honorary degree at Fordham. At the President's dinner afterwards the chair to my right was empty as the meal began. The place card read 'Mr Death'. As soup was served I awaited this gentleman's arrival with a giddy mixture of anxiety and amusement …

PERFORMER: If you were a funeral.

[*The Perfectionist sits in his chair, transfixed by the Puritan.*]

PURITAN: When he finally arrived Mr Death was a nondescript little man with round, pink cheeks and a neat moustache.

He sat down beside me as the waiter was taking my soup bowl, extended a rather large hand before I'd said a word. 'Mr Gould,' he sang, 'my apologies, rush hour traffic, I'm John Deeth.' He pronounced it *'deeth'*.

[*He turns his attention to the Performer and the Perfectionist, tuning them in.*]

PERFORMER: If you were a funeral?

[*Still no reaction from the Perfectionist.*]

PURITAN: And I can remember thinking: this poor little man! Forced to live, day in and day out, with the dreaded fact of that last name. 'Hello, I'm John Deeth. Pleased to meet you, John Deeth. I'm John Deeth. Yes, *Deeth*.' And sooner or later every day he'd have to spell it for somebody and they'd say, Oh, you mean like 'death'? And he'd have to say, No, *deeth*.

PERFORMER: [*to Perfectionist*] A *funeral.*

PURITAN: The helpless daily horror of finding oneself caught in that act of self-deception … and no escape from the pain of it, *ever.*

PERFORMER: A state occasion?

[*Still no reaction from the Perfectionist.*]

PURITAN: Human tragedy is born in a sequence of small daily falsehoods, Mr Deeth. Take my advice, don't base your life on a mispronunciation. Be brave. Be joyfully who you are. Embrace the contradictions.

[*He pulls the blanket around himself and dozes off again.*]

Goodnight … Mr Death.

[*Another note from the ground bass. The Prodigy appears, looking down at the Puritan.*]

PERFORMER: If you were a body, how would you be presented?

PERFECTIONIST: Unadorned. One vase of calla lilies.

PERFORMER: And what would be the text for the service?

PERFECTIONIST: Something from Revelations. A reading

from *Burnt Norton*. And then the final aria from the Goldberg Variations.

[*The Performer becomes aware of the Puritan for the first time.*]

PERFORMER: And how will the congregation respond?

PERFECTIONIST: There will be moments of incandescent grief. The music going up and up and up. The mourners feeling that they too are part of this great unfinished journey. Canadians are a curious breed, you see. They find unity in their sense of collective loss.

PERFORMER: A *Canadian* funeral?

PERFECTIONIST: Yes. Oh yes. Very much so. *Shh.*

[*The Perfectionist, Performer and Prodigy hold the tableau around the Puritan's inert form. Lights fade. Another note from the ground bass.*]

Variation 30: The Quodlibet

[*Sound: telephone rings. The Puritan rouses himself from his sleep. Picks up the phone. The other players react with surprise to this resurrection.*]

PURITAN: Hello, Jessie. No, I'm feeling fine! I am heading into my 'late period', Jessie. With luck and pluck it may span the next twenty-five years. I have so many plans. I am going to give up recording, stay away from the piano entirely and work on my skills as a conductor. I am going to compose – I have a wonderful idea for a piece based on the Book of Revelations. But before all that I am going to return to the concert stage for one final performance, live before an audience of dignitaries on an oil rig in the Arctic Ocean! You think I'm kidding! I've already recorded it!

[*Music sting: the opening guitar riff from 'Sgt Pepper's Lonely Hearts Club Band'. The Performer breaks loose from his strait-jacket and starts to boogie.*]

PERFECTIONIST: [*entering, cueing out the music*] Cut the mop tops! I *need* music, not this clichéd rubbish! Chopin, Schumann and Liszt are definitely a waste of time!

[*A mish-mash of classical music plays, under.*]

PURITAN: [*raising his voice over the interruption*] All kidding aside, Jessie, I have an enormous compulsion to winter over in the Canadian Arctic.

[*The Performer starts to skip using the sleeves of his strait-jacket as a rope. He sings a Petula Clark medley.*]

PERFORMER: [*under*] 'It's a sign of the times / That my love for you is getting so much stronger!'

PERFECTIONIST: Schubert can be tolerated occasionally! All of the early Romantics can go jump in the lake except Mendelssohn.

[*He whirls around and begins to conduct an invisible orchestra.*]

PERFORMER: [*under*] 'When you're alone / And life is making you lonely / You can always go – Downtown.' 'I close my eyes and I can fly / And I escape from all this worldly strife / Restricted by routine of life / But still I can't discover: Who am I?'

PURITAN: [*over*] The mental state I must struggle to maintain living here in the south occurs as a natural human response to the pure physical reality of the far north! [*to the Perfectionist*] Keep it down!

PERFECTIONIST: Verdi, Puccini and the other operatic masters are trained poodles! I despise Debussy, Ravel and Poulenc!

PERFORMER: [*overlapping Perfectionist*] 'My love is warmer than the warmest sunshine / Softer than a sigh / My love is deeper than the deepest ocean / Wider than the sky.'

PERFECTIONIST: [*overlapping Performer*] Stravinsky and Bartok are the two most over-rated composers of the century! Mozart, what can I tell you about Mozart? Elevator music!

[*suddenly aware of the Performer*] Pet Clark! Now there's a little lady who had her head screwed on!

PURITAN: Control yourself!

> [*The Performer stops singing Petula Clark. The musical mish-mash fades to Strauss underscore. The Prodigy tears a sheet off the Puritan's pad and reads it breathlessly. The Performer reads over his shoulder. They carry on, overlapped by the Puritan and the Perfectionist.*]

PRODIGY: Glenn Gould: Alter egos of. As animal lover.

PERFORMER: Artistic legacy of. Back injury of. Career of. Cars of. As celebrity. Chair built for.

PRODIGY: Concert career abandoned by.

PERFORMER: Counterpoint as preoccupation of.

PRODIGY: Critics disliked by. Depression suffered by.

PERFORMER: Devotion needed by. Eccentricities of. Fan letters to. First experience of booing by.

PRODIGY: Flying feared by. Games enjoyed by. Health problems of. Honours awarded to.

PURITAN: [*overlapping Prodigy, above*] I'd like to set up a puppy farm on Manitoulin Island – a home for the all the unwanted doggies in the world. A farmhouse in a February field, grey light dissolving into grey land, and guess who is going to live there with me, Jessie?

> [*He smiles.*]

PERFORMER: Hymns loved by.

PRODIGY: Insomnia suffered by. As International star. Isolation of. Left-handedness of.

PERFORMER: Memorization skills of. Money earned by.

PRODIGY: Newspaper written by, in childhood. Perfect pitch of. Persona of. As Prodigy ...

> [*He pauses, studies his hands. Sound: Arctic wind.*]

PURITAN: [*to Jessie*] Finally, I have an enormous compulsion to gaze upon the Polar seas, Jessie. The wind has not touched another face. It is your wind. The day is your day. The sky is the crown of your head.

PERFECTIONIST: I prefer the model of Richard Strauss – a man who made much richer his own time by not being part of it. Who spoke of all generations by being of none.

PURITAN: The Goldbergs are finished now. The total ordering of sound in time. Unity. Coherence. Structure. These are the things that have mattered most to us. To become one with the Absolute and become aware of that oneness –

[*The Prodigy smiles.*]

PERFECTIONIST: – inside merging with outside ... in the divine architecture of the sublime.

[*He hesitates in his moment of hara kiri, summoning his resolve.*]

PRODIGY: As Performer ...

[*The Performer looks at the Perfectionist.*]

PERFORMER: A pulse of intense feeling that illuminated the means of its own transmission.

PRODIGY: As Perfectionist ...

PERFORMER: I looked for a truth outside myself ... and finding it, became part of the truth I sought ...

PRODIGY: As Puritan ...

[*The Prodigy and the Performer turn their attention to the Puritan. He touches finger to forehead – the 'I know' gesture.*]

PURITAN: These are the happiest days of my life, Jessie! I have had a revolution in my head.

[*Sudden startle. The onset of seizure.*]

I can feel ... the blood ... in my brain.

[*The other Glenns touch finger to forehead. Lights fade to black. Another note from the ground bass.*]

The Final Aria

[*Music up: Final Aria, late version. The four players move across the stage in half-light, conducting themselves in time to the music as the lights fade. They turn once, eyes uplifted to Bach's cathedral, and continue their slow exit, raising one hand to conduct the last notes of the Aria as the lights fade down to black.*]

Edited for the press by damian lopes

Design by damian lopes and Stan Bevington
Cover design by Rick/Simon

Typeset in Cartier Book. In January 1967 the graphic designer Carl Dair released Cartier, the first typeface to be designed in Canada. In 1998, Rod McDonald reworked the roman, finished the italic and added a bold weight. He incorporated many changes necessary to produce a working text face for digital typesetting.

To read the online version of this text and other titles from Coach House Books, or to order any of our titles, visit our website: www.chbooks.com

To add your name to our e-mailing list, write to: mail@chbooks.com   Phone toll-free: 1 800 367 6360

Coach House Books
80 bpNichol Lane
Toronto Ontario M5S 3J7